Oak Bookcase, designed by Harvey Ellis and executed by Gustav Stickley

THE EARLY WORK OF
GUSTAV STICKLEY

by

Stephen Gray

Published by

TURN of the CENTURY EDITIONS

250 West Broadway
New York, N.Y. 10013

ISBN 0940326-08-6

Oak Corner China Cabinet with Leaded Glass from the Craftsman Workshops

CONTENTS

*Photographs of Craftsman Furniture designed by Harvey Ellis,
courtesy of Nancy A. McClelland, Christie's, New York...pp. 2, 6, 72, 116, 138 & 174.*

*Photographs of twelve tile Grueby table and Craftsman copper and glass chandelier,
courtesy of Marilee B. Meyer, Robert W. Skinner, Inc...pp. 73 & 148.*

*Photograph of early Gustav Stickley corner china closet with leaded glass,
courtesy of Michael Carey...p. 4.*

- - - - - - - -

*"New Furniture from the Workshop of Gustav Stickley" courtesy of
Mary Anne Clegg Smith of Fayetteville, New York.*

1902 Retail Plates courtesy of Richard Sagendorph of Spencer, Massachusetts.

*1909 "Handwrought Metal Work from the Craftsman Workshops", courtesy of
Mr. & Mrs. William Porter of Birmingham, Michigan.*

*Inlaid Oak Armchair with "Shoe" Feet, designed by Harvey Ellis
and executed by Gustav Stickley*

INTRODUCTION

"The Early Work of Gustav Stickley", the eighth in a series devoted to American Arts and Crafts furnishings, is a valuable adjunct to *The Collected Works of Gustav Stickley*. This volume is a compilation of photos and drawings from original catalogs and other source material published by Gustav Stickley's Craftsman Workshop. We have emphasized the earliest examples of his furniture and present them arranged in the chronological order of publication. Also, an extensive selection of lamps, shades, hanging fixtures and pieces made of wicker are illustrated. We have taken the liberty of reorganizing many of the items and catalog pages to aid clarity and appearance. In addition, some contemporary photos of rare and exceptional examples made prior to 1905 are included.

In 1900, with Catalog No. 1 "New Furniture", Gustav Stickley introduced his line of Arts and Crafts furniture to the public. At the Grand Rapids trade show in July of that year, George Clingman of Tobey Furniture bought Stickley's production and marketed it as his own from the same catalog with the Tobey Company logo on the cover but with no mention whatsoever of Gustav Stickley. The omission may have helped motivate Stickley to market his own furniture. Thereafter, he would distribute his furniture to retailers clearly marked with his logo, to be sold with or without a store label. A list of outlets across America distributing the furniture was featured prominently in the "Craftsman Magazine".

The next section reproduces the loose portfolio sheets and excerpts from the pamphlet entitled from "Chips from the Craftsman Workshops", which was issued in 1901. We suspect all of these pieces of furniture were actually built, and examples of most of them have surfaced today. The original finish combined with the patination that results from age adds to their visual appeal and economic value. The drawings cannot justly express the richness of color, nor do they capture the beauty of woodgrain and the exquisite structural detail that make these designs so arresting. As Gustav Stickley often stated, the finish and selection of wood are essential elements to the design of Craftsman furniture. Stickley felt so strongly about the positive visual effect of quarter-sawn oak that on occasion he used thick veneer to face the legs of Morris chairs, settles, and dining tables and the sides of some serving pieces.

We next present a series of plates that were printed in 1902 and distributed to large retailers to help customers select items from the Craftsman Workshop that may not have been on display. This group of photographs represents Stickley's first coherent assemblage of manufactured furniture featuring all the basic designs.

In early 1903, Stickley hired Rochester, New York, architect Harvey Ellis. By this time, Ellis had a respected but blemished reputation (he was a reckless individualist and an alcoholic) among architects as an innovator attuned to the emerging Prairie Style. In hiring Ellis, Stickley continued an integration of Arts and Crafts influences with the idea of creating a true Craftsman style. Ellis extended Stickley's range in furniture design, and was also instrumental in broadening Stickley's vocabulary to include interior and exterior architectural treatments fulfilling his Arts and Crafts ideal. Although Ellis died in January 1904, after having worked only seven months for Stickley, his designs forever changed the Craftsman esthetic. The influence of Harvey Ellis is apparent in many examples shown in "Catalog D", which introduced less massive pieces of furniture featuring inlay, wide sweeping curves, broad overhangs and outwardly bowed sides. The more sophisticated and affluent people of that time found these forms, especially the inlaid pieces, most appealing. They reflected international design developments that were already well recognized in the work of Charles Rennie Mackintosh, Charles F.A. Voysey, Josef Hoffmann and others. One of the most important goals of the guild, the United Crafts, that Stickley established in Eastwood, New York, was "to substitute the luxury of taste for the luxury of costliness, to place within the reach of the middle class purchaser, articles of practical use, which are at the same time, works of art". The realities of commerce and the influence of Harvey Ellis imparted additional breadth to Stickley's work. Structural integrity, functionalism and lack of embellishment were no longer enough to satisfy the demand of Stickley's burgeoning clientele.

The next section presents the "Supplement to Catalog D", an addendum to "Catalog D", as reprinted in *The Collected Works of Gustav Stickley*. Spindle furniture was first introduced here in 1905. The public's taste began to change and Stickley reacted by producing furniture built "on rather lighter lines", which was also less expensive, easier to handle, and better suited to smaller rooms.

We hope this book will expand existing knowledge and answer questions regarding the production and design of Gustav Stickley's Craftsman Furniture between 1901 and 1909. When examined carefully, the evolution and development of the Craftsman Style can be followed. The prediction by Gustav Stickley of the value and durability of his furniture for future generations has certainly proven to be correct.

Stephen Gray
September, 1987

CATALOG NO. 1 "NEW FURNITURE"

The furniture Gustav Stickley introduced in Catalog No. 1, "New Furniture", is the earliest expression of an emerging American Arts and Crafts style that is indebted to various historical and cultural influences. Harking back to an earlier time, Stickley sought inspiration in the Alpine chalet, Tudor cottage, Japanese teahouse and Spanish mission. Yet, his imperative to simplify and remove superfluous ornamentation, appears in these early pieces. Some examples relate to traditional designs from regions of Europe and Asia. In others, a sense of Stickley's experiment with Art Nouveau is distinctly evident, as in the conventionalized plant forms used in some of the earlier selections. The "mission" furniture shown in this section acknowledges designs emanating from the new social awareness that was evolving in the United States and abroad.

Bombay
Plant Stand
   Number 8
Height 21 inche
Grueby Tile
Top

Damascus Plant Stand
Grueby Tile Top
   Height, 21 inches
      Number 9

India Plant Stand
   Number 7 Tile Top
   Number 7½ Wood Top
      21 inches high

Chalet
Plant
Stand
   No. 6
Grueby
Tile Top
   No. 6½
Wood top
Height
21 inches

Mikado Plant Stand
Grueby Tile Top
20 inches high
12⅜ inch top
Number 13

Yeddo Plant
Stand
Grueby Tile
in Top
24 inches high
14½ inch top
Number 11

Tokio Plant Stand
Grueby Tile Top
Number 10
Height, 21⅝ inches
Top, 14 in. square

Yokohama Plant Stand
Grueby Tile Top
19 inches high
12⅜ inch top
Number 12

**Bellworth Tabourette
Number 1
Top, 18 inches
Height, 20 inches**

**Poppy Table Number 26
Top, 20 inches
Height, 23 inches**

**Twin-Flower Tabourette
Number 3
Height, 19¼ inches
Top, 17½ inches**

**Sunflower Tea-Table
Number 32
Height, 22 inches
Top, 22 inches**

Foxglove Tabourette
Height, 23¼ inches
Top, 19 inches
Number 2

The Adder Tabourette
Number 33
Height, 23 inches
Top, 22⅜ inches

Tom Jones
Drink Stand
Height, 30 inches
Number 98

Lotos Tabourette
Number 28
Top, 19 inches
Height, 20 inches

𝔗𝔬𝔪 𝔍𝔬𝔫𝔢𝔰
𝔇𝔯𝔦𝔫𝔨 𝔖𝔱𝔞𝔫𝔡
𝔥𝔢𝔦𝔤𝔥𝔱, 30 𝔦𝔫𝔠𝔥𝔢𝔰
𝔑𝔲𝔪𝔟𝔢𝔯 99

𝔠𝔢𝔩𝔞𝔫𝔡𝔦𝔫𝔢 𝔗𝔢𝔞
𝔗𝔞𝔟𝔩𝔢
𝔑𝔲𝔪𝔟𝔢𝔯 27
24 𝔦𝔫𝔠𝔥𝔢𝔰 𝔥𝔦𝔤𝔥
𝔗𝔬𝔭, 20 𝔦𝔫𝔠𝔥𝔢𝔰

𝔐𝔞𝔩𝔩𝔬𝔴 𝔗𝔢𝔞 𝔗𝔞𝔟𝔩𝔢
𝔑𝔲𝔪𝔟𝔢𝔯 34
22¼ 𝔦𝔫𝔠𝔥𝔢𝔰 𝔥𝔦𝔤𝔥
22¾ 𝔦𝔫𝔠𝔥 𝔱𝔬𝔭

𝔓𝔞𝔫𝔰𝔶 𝔗𝔢𝔞 𝔗𝔞𝔟𝔩𝔢
𝔑𝔲𝔪𝔟𝔢𝔯 29
22 𝔦𝔫𝔠𝔥𝔢𝔰 𝔥𝔦𝔤𝔥
24-𝔦𝔫𝔠𝔥 𝔱𝔬𝔭

Chalet Tabourette
21 inches long
16½ inches high
Number 22

Chalet Table
Large Size, No. 402
30 inches High
30-inch Top
Small Size, No. 403
22 inches High
24-inch Top

Bungalow Tables
Number 5½
31 inches high
30-inch top

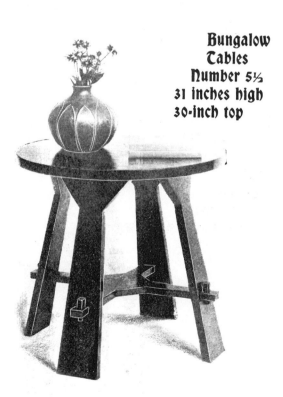

Bungalow Plant Stand
Number 19
18 inches high

Tea Table
24 inches high
24-inch top
Number 5

Tabourette
Number 4
Height, 18 inches
Top, 18 inches

Club
Tabourette
No. 16
18 in. high
18-in. top

Club
Tables
No. 17
24 in. high
24-in. top

No. 18
30 in. high
30-in. top

Cottage Plant Stand
Tile Top, Number 20
Wood Top, Number 21
21½ inches high
18-inch top

Number 14
Cottage Pedestal
30 inches high
Number 15
Cottage
Plant Stand
21½ inches high

Cottage Plant
Stand
Number 21
21½ inches high
18-inch top

Number 700
Spanish Leather
Stool
20¼ inches long

Chalet Seat
Number 709
Spanish Leather
24 inches wide

Chalet Stool
Number 709
25½ inches long
17 inches high
Spanish Leather
Austrian Oak

Bench   Number 702
Length, 21¼ inches

Cottage Seats

Number 716
16 inches high
Top 19 inches square

Number 718
18 inches high
Top 19 inches square

India Seat
Number 797

Leather Covered Seat
Number 701
Height, 16½ inches
Length, 21 inches

Manor Hall Seats
Double—No. 154
36 inches long
Single—No. 151
25 inches long

Number 704
Manor
Plant Stand
Length, 21½ inches

Manor Hall Seats
Single—No. 152
25 inches long
Double—No. 155
36 inches long
Spanish Leather

Smokers' Cabinet
24¾ inches high
Number 501

Smokers' Cabinet
24¼ inches high
Number 502

Chalet Smokers' Cabinet
Height, 27¾ inches
Number 503

Chalet Bench
Number 156
19 inches high
30 inches long

Chalet Bench
Number 157
19 inches high
29¼ inches long

Bungalow Library Table
Number 401
Austrian Oak
Top, 30 x 48 inches

Piano Bench
Length,
Height,
Number 160

Piano Bench
Length,
Height,
Number 159

Bungalow
Library
Table
Top, 30 x 48 in.
Number 404

**Venetian
Pedestal
Number 25
32¼ inches
in height**

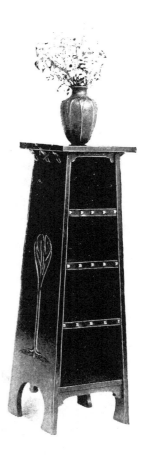

**Chalet
Magazine
Cabinet
43¼ inches high
Number 500**

**Spanish Arm Chair
Number 2576
Made in Oak
Leather Seat**

Bungalow Library
Chair
    Number 2556

Bungalow
Rocker
    Number
    2555

**Bungalow
Dining
Chair
Rush Seat
    Number
    1289**

**Manor Hall Seats
    Single—No. 153½
Length, 25 inches
    Double—No. 150½
    Length 36 inches
    Rush Seat**

**Bungalow
Arm
Chair
    Rush
    Seat
        Number
        1289A**

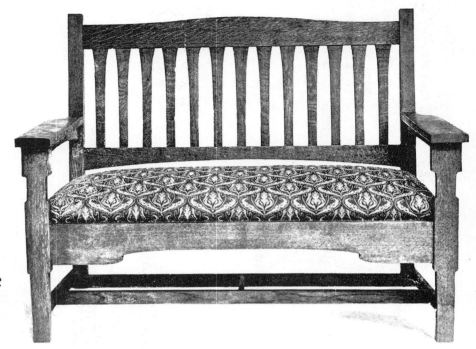

Bungalow Settee Number 2556T

Bungalow Settee with Rush Seat Number 1289T

Chalet Desk (closed)
Number 505

Chalet Desk (open)
Height, 46 inches
Width, 23½ inches
Number 505

Chalet Desk Stool
Height, 16 inches
Top, 14 x 17 inches

Chalet Desk Chair
Rush Seat
Number 2578

This photograph appeared in "Chips from the Workshops of the United Crafts"
and distributed by Cobb-Eastman Co., Boston, MA.

CHIPS FROM THE WORKSHOP OF GUSTAV STICKLEY

In 1901 when this document was published, Gustav Stickley had already become a widely recognized, independent furniture maker. This pamphlet was actually an Arts and Crafts manifesto, interspersed with sketches of furniture. A detailed price list with accurate dimensions and style numbers was inserted as an addendum. In creating this furniture, Stickley was concerned with the choice of material, care used in construction and the consideration of function and beauty. He clearly favored fumed oak, but it did not end there. "The look of age is intensified by staining in tints and applying a soft, dull finish. Oak treated in this manner might well pass for the unaided work of nature and time". Grueby tiles, practical for washstands, plant stands, and tabourets are specifically mentioned as an aid in creating artistic effects. He found spots of intense color on a negative background of dark oak most effective. Natural rush seats and hides of leather appropriately toned also served as an adjunct to the woods.

By 1901, Stickley felt his furniture was distinctive in design and that it clearly deviated from established forms. The break with Art Nouveau and the Aesthetic Movement was established by the "perfect correspondence of the piece to its primitive use and intention". Historic styles were abandoned and an evolution of form occurred that clearly placed Gustav Stickley at the forefront of the Modern Movement as it has become known today. Through travel abroad, international expositions, and publications, ideas were exchanged, absorbed, and expressed by the designers and craftsmen of that period.

Chips
FROM THE WORKSHOPS OF THE
United Crafts
EASTWOOD N.Y
U.S.A

The Craftsman, February 1902

The Craftsman, May 1902

SECRETARY № 515

CHAIR № 1297

DIVAN Nº 161
HEIGHT 39" WIDTH 52"

DIVAN Nº 165
HEIGHT 40" LENGTH 60" DEPTH 26"

FOOT STOOL Nº 726

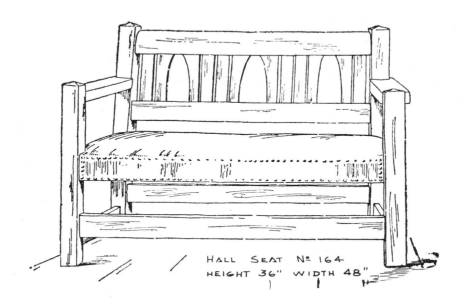

HALL SEAT No 164
HEIGHT 36" WIDTH 48"

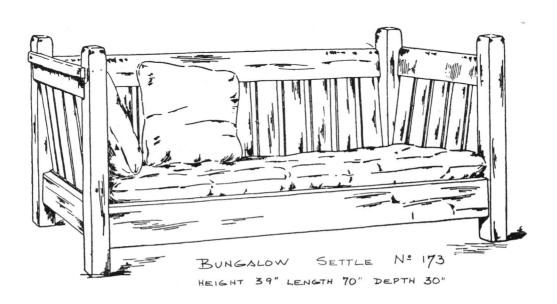

BUNGALOW SETTLE No 173
HEIGHT 39" LENGTH 70" DEPTH 30"

DIVAN № 170
HEIGHT 27" LENTH 52" DEPTH 28"

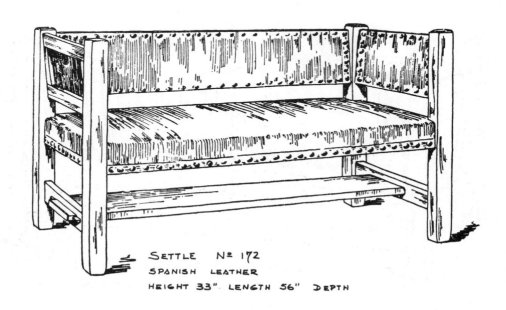

SETTLE № 172
SPANISH LEATHER
HEIGHT 33" LENGTH 56" DEPTH

HALL SETTLE Nº 163
HEIGHT 56" WIDTH 56"

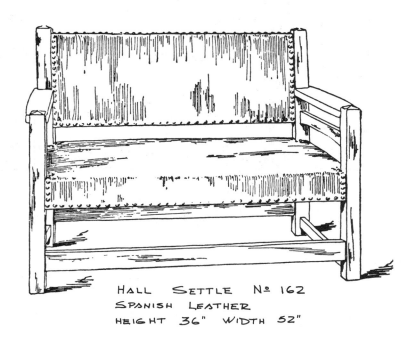

HALL SETTLE Nº 162
SPANISH LEATHER
HEIGHT 36" WIDTH 52"

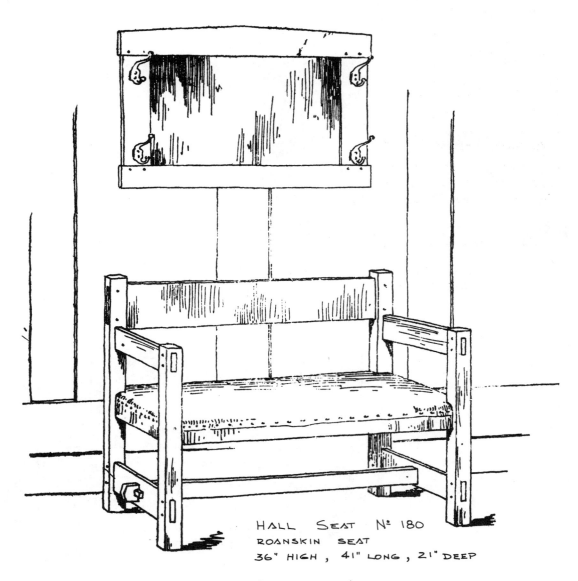

HALL SEAT Nº 180
ROANSKIN SEAT
36" HIGH , 41" LONG , 21" DEEP

MIRROR Nº 608
26" HIGH , 36" LONG

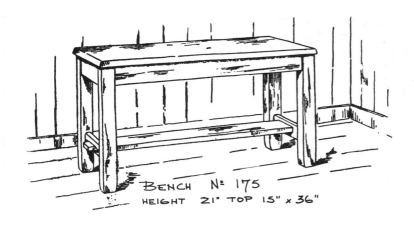

BENCH No 175
HEIGHT 21" TOP 15" x 36"

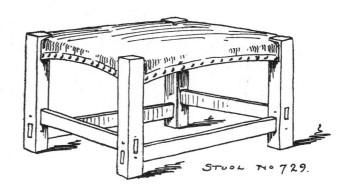

STOOL No 729.

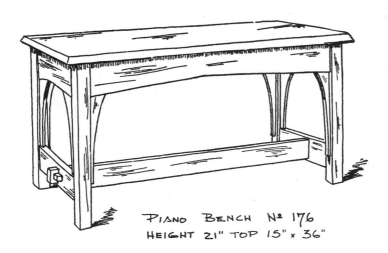

PIANO BENCH No 176
HEIGHT 21" TOP 15" x 36"

SMOKERS CABINET
Nº 502

FIRE SIDE Nº 178
HEIGHT 27" SEAT 18" x 36"

WINDOW SEAT Nº 177
SPANISH LEATHER
HEIGHT 27" SEAT 18" x 26"

STOOL Nº 728
HEIGHT 18" SIZE 18" x 18"

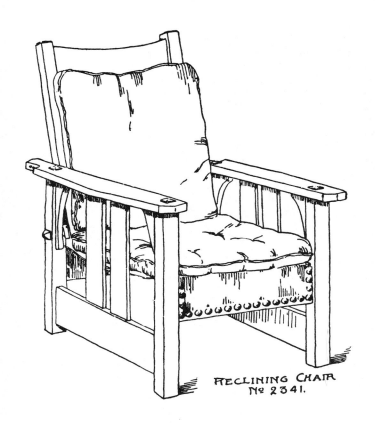

RECLINING CHAIR
Nº 2341.

RECLINING CHAIR
Nº 2340

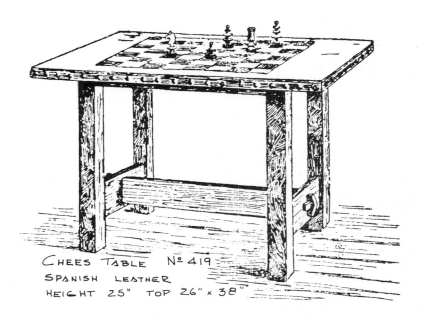

CHEES TABLE   No 419
SPANISH LEATHER
HEIGHT 25"   TOP 26" x 38"

MAGAZINE CABINET No 514
HEIGHT 44" WIDTH 12" DEPTH 15"

MAGAZINE
CABINET
No 506

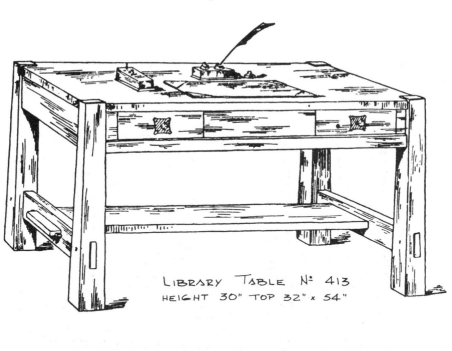

LIBRARY TABLE N° 413
HEIGHT 30" TOP 32" x 54"

ARM·CHAIR N° 2576

WRITING TABLE N° 417
WITH DRAWER & LOCKERS
COVERED WITH SPANISH LEATHER
SCREEN N° 102

LIBRARY TABLE N° 409
COVERED WITH SPANISH LEATHER
TOP 36 x 60 INCHES.
LEATHER SCREEN N° 101.

LIBRARY TABLE Nº 410
COVERED WITH SPANISH LEATHER
HEIGHT 30", HEXAGONAL TOP 48"

LIBRARY TABLE № 420
HEIGHT 30" TOP 40" DIAMETER

LIBRARY TABLE № 407
HEIGHT 30" TOP 48 DIAMETER

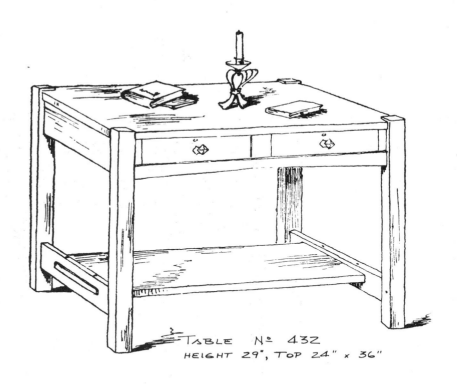

Table No 432
HEIGHT 29", TOP 24" x 36"

LIBRARY TABLE No 404
HEIGHT 30", TOP 30" x 48"

WRITTING TABLE Nº 416
HEIGHT 30" TOP 26" x 42"

TABLE DESK Nº 430
HEIGHT 29" TOP 24" x 36"

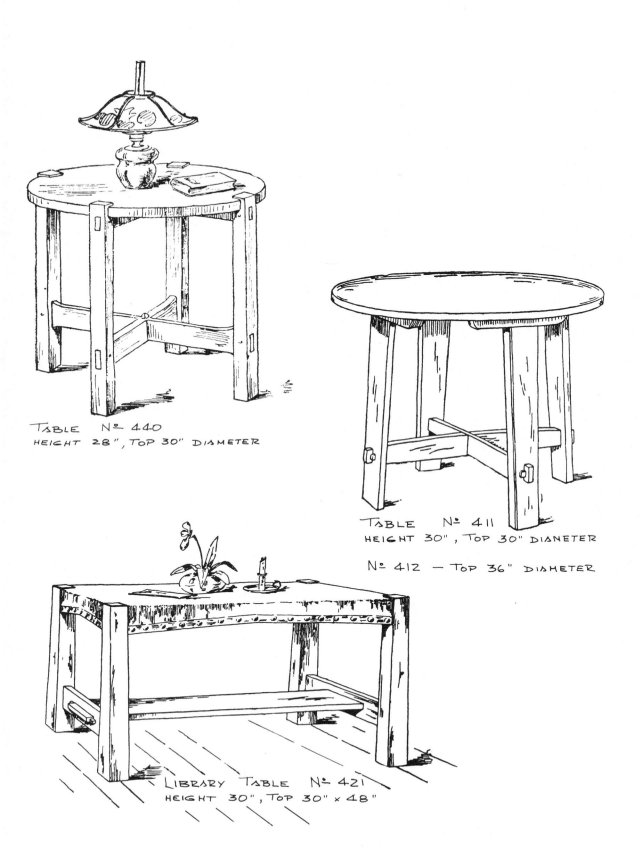

TABLE   N⁰ 440
HEIGHT 28", TOP 30" DIAMETER

TABLE   N⁰ 411
HEIGHT 30", TOP 30" DIAMETER

N⁰ 412 — TOP 36" DIAMETER

LIBRARY TABLE   N⁰ 421
HEIGHT 30", TOP 30" x 48"

TEA TABLE No 426
HEIGHT 26" TOP 23" x 40"

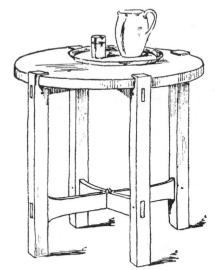

DRINK TABLE No 136
HEIGHT 28" TOP 24" DIAMETER

BREAKFAST TABLE No 441
HEIGHT 30", TOP 36" DIAMETER

TEA TABLE No 439
HEIGHT 26", TOP 26" DIAMETER

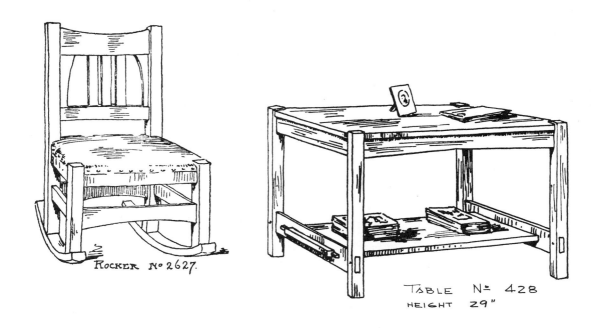

ROCKER No 2627.

TABLE No 428
HEIGHT 29"

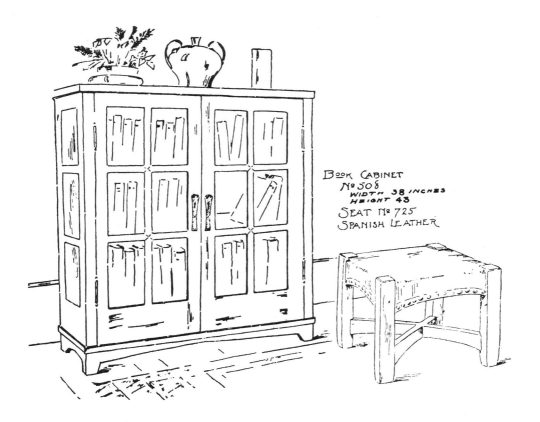

BOOK CABINET
No 508
WIDTH 38 INCHES
HEIGHT 43
SEAT No 725
SPANISH LEATHER

BOOK CABINET No 525
HEIGHT 56", WIDTH 42", DEPTH 12"

BOOK CABINET
No 508.

BOOK CABINET № 512
HEIGHT 38" WIDTH 30" DEPTH 12"

BOOK CASE No 510

CHINA CABINET N° 902
HEIGHT 64" WIDTH 36" DEPTH 16"
AUSTRIAN OAK AND GREEN ASH

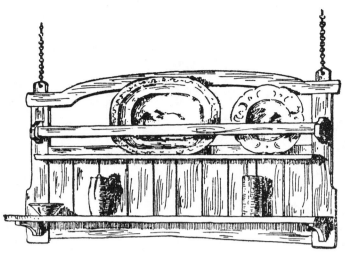

PLATE RACK N° 903
HEIGHT 20" WIDTH 46"

SIDE BOARD N° 901
HEIGHT 36" TOP 23" x 50"
BACK 40" IN HIGH

DINING TABLE No. 418
HEIGHT 30" TOP 60" DIAMETER

DINING CHAIR No. 1296

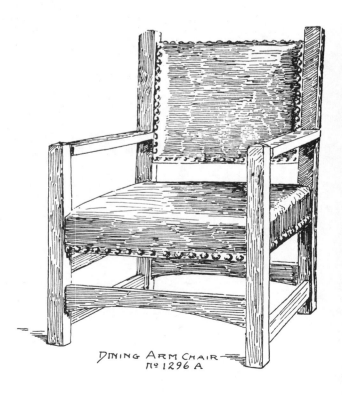

DINING ARM CHAIR
No. 1296 A

DINING ARM CHAIR
Nº 1291 A

DINING CHAIR
Nº 1291.

LUNCH TABLE Nº 424
TOP 28 × 40 INCHES.

ARM CHAIR Nº 2612.

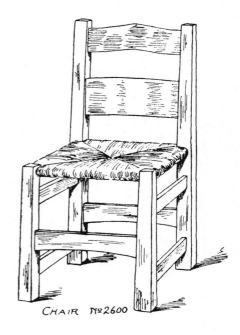

CHAIR Nº 2600

DINING CHAIR
Nº 1299

CHAIR Nº 2578

Dining Arm Chair
No 1292.

Dining Chair
No 1292.

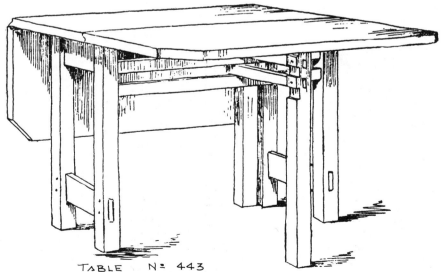

TABLE   No 443
DROP LEAF TABLE, OAK, WOOD TOP.
30" HIGH, TOP 40" x 42"

DINNER GONG
AUSTRIAN OAK AND GREEN ASK
HEIGHT 37" WIDTH 24" GONG 18"

TABOURET   Nº 45
HEIGHT 21" TOP 16"

TABOURET   Nº 46
HEIGHT 21" TOP 19"

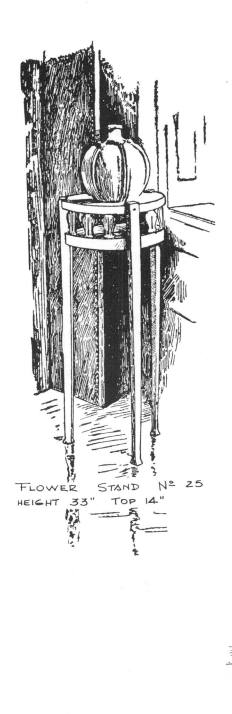

FLOWER STAND N° 25
HEIGHT 33" TOP 14"

PLANT STAND N° 48
HEIGHT 30" TOP 11" x 11"

PLANT STAND N° 44
HEIGHT 30" TOP 13" x 13"

ARM CHAIR Nº 2582.
ROAN-SKIN SEAT

ROCKER Nº 2581
ROAN-SKIN SEAT.

ARM CHAIR Nº 2590
ROAN SKIN SEAT

ARM CHAIR
Nº 2576
HEAVY SPANISH LEATHER

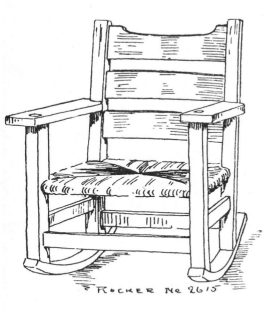

ROCKER No 2615

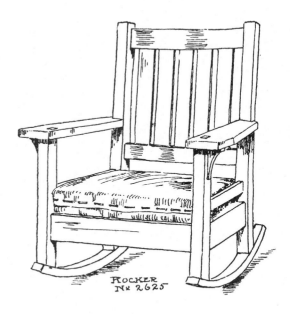

ROCKER No 2625

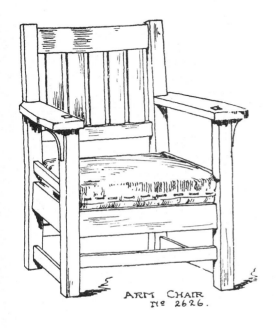

ARM CHAIR No 2626.

ROCKER No 2635

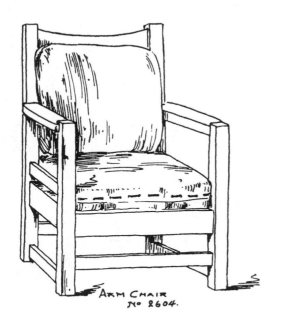

ARM CHAIR
No 2604.

ROCKER No. 2603.

LIBRARY CHAIR No 2594
HEAVY SPANISH LEATHER

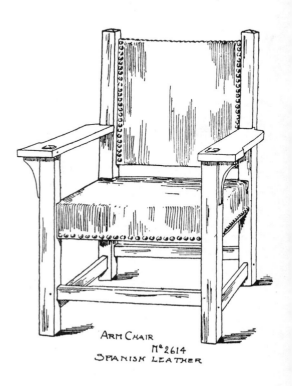

ARM CHAIR
No 2614
SPANISH LEATHER

ARM CHAIR Nº 2592

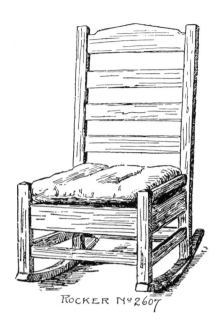

ROCKER Nº 2607

READING CHAIR Nº 2596.

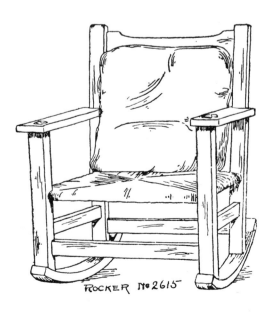

ROCKER Nº 2615

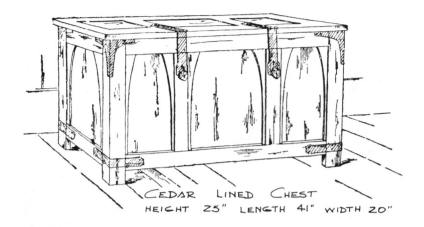

CEDAR LINED CHEST
HEIGHT 25" LENGTH 41" WIDTH 20"

CHEST OF DRAWERS No 602
HEIGHT 48" TOP 20" x 40"

SAMBO Nº 605
HEIGHT 30" TOP 16" x 13"

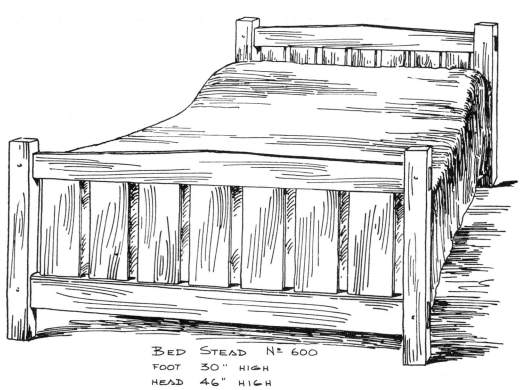

BED STEAD Nº 600
FOOT 30" HIGH
HEAD 46" HIGH

PLATE N° 102
GLASS CABINET
SERVING BOARD

PLATE N° 302
SETTLE WITH CHEST
TABLE COVERED WITH
SPANISH LEATHER
HALL GLASS.

PLATE NO 13
TABLE - TOP COVERED
WITH SPANISH LEATHER
SMALL TABLE
WINDOW SEAT

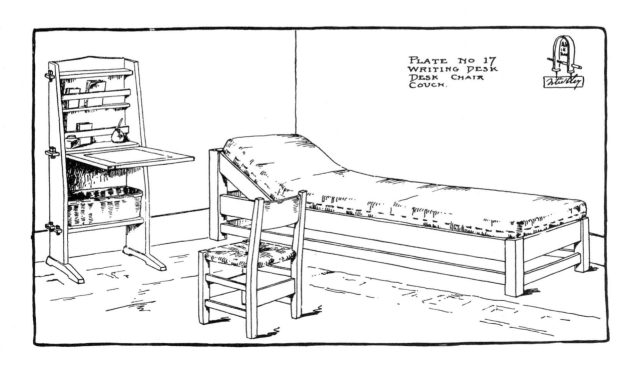

PLATE NO 17
WRITING DESK
DESK CHAIR
COUCH.

Oak and Wrought-iron Secretary, designed by Harvey Ellis and executed by Gustav Stickley

RETAIL PLATES PUBLISHED BY GUSTAV STICKLEY IN 1902

By 1902, Gustav Stickley had passed through a period of development and experimentation at United Crafts. It was there he formed a Guild of cabinet makers, metal workers, and leather workers that brought the Craftsman ideals of household art to its fullest expression. The following plates were from a series of photographs taken of the actual pieces being offered for sale. In wide use at the time, only two partial sets of these pictures seem to have survived. The furniture shown in this section is Gustav Stickley at his best—hardy, confident, and powerfully elegant. The later considerations of changing taste, cost of material and need for greater production had not impacted on the purity of these designs. Differences can be seen clearly when these plates are compared to "Catalog D", printed in 1904 and reprinted in *The Collected Works of Gustav Stickley.*

Oak and Twelve Tile Grueby Tea Table from the Craftsman Workshops

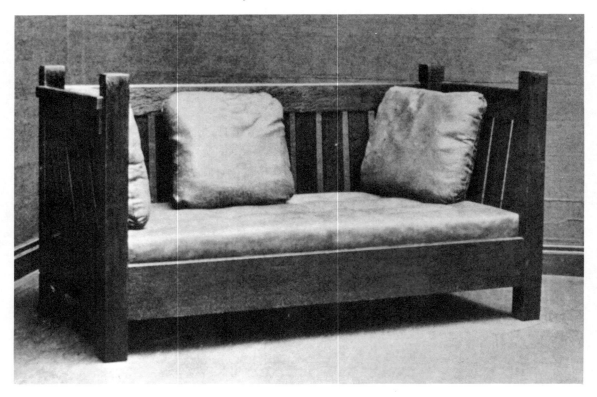

SETTLE No. 173
39" high. 70" long, 30" deep

SETTLE No. 188
36" high, 84" long, 34" deep

DIVAN NO. 165
    40″ high, 60″ long, 26″ deep

STOOL No. 725
    17″ high, 17″ wide, 20″ long

SETTLE No. 189
    47″ high, 84″ long, 34″ deep

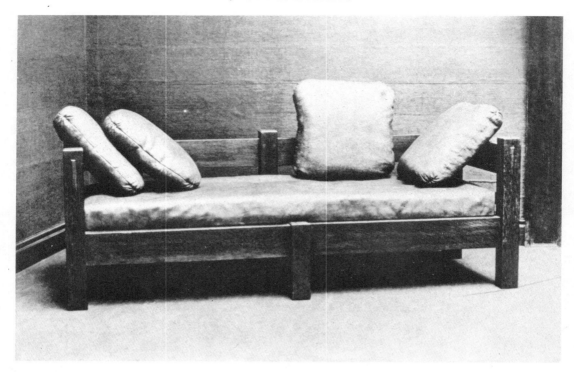

SETTLE No. 171
27" high, 72" long, 30" deep

SETTLE No. 169
36" high, 78" long, 38" deep

HALL SEAT No. 196

56" high, 70" long, 25" deep

SETTLE No. 161

39" high, 52" long, 25" deep
Seat cushion in Soft Leather

HALL SEAT No. 186
    39″ high, 48″ long, 22″ deep

ARM CHAIR No. 1299-A
ARM ROCKER No. 2637

HALL SEAT No. 182
    37″ high, 49″ long, 25″ deep
    Chest under seat

ARM ROCKER No. 2615

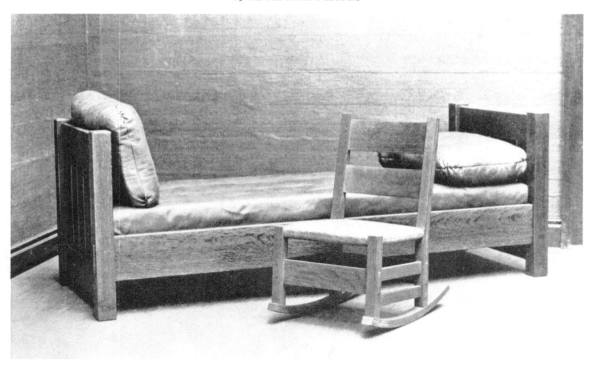

LOUNGE No. 191

29" high, 74" long, 30" wide

SMALL ROCKER No. 2635

WRITING DESK No. 453

30" high, 22" wide, 40" long

Drawer Pulls of wrought iron or copper

DESK CHAIR No. 2578

ARM CHAIR No. 2584
OFFICE CHAIR No. 2584½

ARM ROCKER No. 2625
ARM CHAIR No. 2626

DINING CHAIR No. 1299
DINING ARM CHAIR No. 1299-A

SMALL ROCKER No. 2635
ARM ROCKER No. 2637

SMALL ROCKER No. 2617
SMALL CHAIR No. 2618

ARM ROCKER No. 2615
ARM CHAIR No. 2616

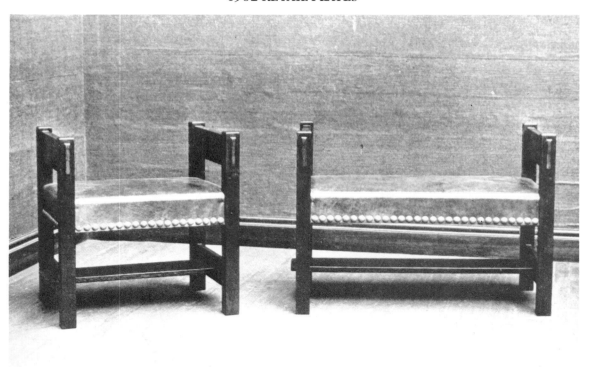

WINDOW SEAT No. 177

27″ high, 26″ long, 18″ wide

WINDOW SEAT No. 178

27″ high, 36″ long, 18″ wide

LIBRARY TABLE No. 421-L

30″ high, 48″ long, 30″ wide

LIBRARY TABLE No. 454

30" high, 36" wide, 66" long
Drawer Pulls of wrought iron or copper

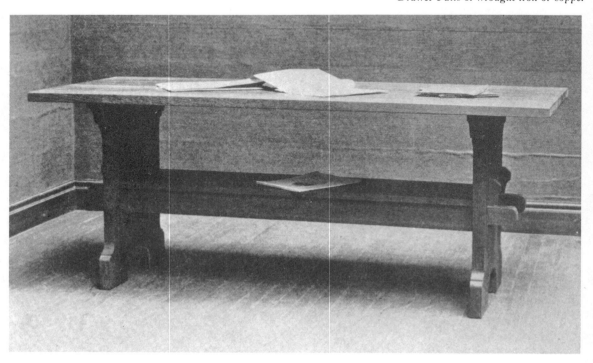

LIBRARY TABLE No. 445
30" high, 70" long, 30" wide

LIBRARY TABLE No. 407

30″ high, top 48″ diameter

ADJUSTABLE-BACK CHAIR No. 2341

LIBRARY TABLE No. 460-L

30″ high, 36″ wide, 66″ long

Drawer Pulls of wrought iron or copper

LIBRARY TABLE No. 433

30″ high, 48″ long, 30″ wide

TABLE No. 456

30″ high, 24″ wide, 36″ long
2 drawers

TABLE No. 424

    30″ high, 28″ wide, 40″ long

SMALL ROCKER No. 2607

SMALL CHAIR No. 2608

LIBRARY TABLE No. 461

    30″ high, 32″ wide, 54″ long
    Drawer Pulls of wrought iron or copper

ARM ROCKER No. 2617-A

ARM CHAIR No. 2618-A

ARM ROCKER No. 2631
ARM CHAIR No. 2632

ARM ROCKER No. 2597
ARM CHAIR No. 2598

STOOL No. 194
17" high, 24" long, 30" wide
ARM CHAIR No. 2592

LIBRARY TABLE No. 401
30" high, 30" wide, 48" long
SIDE CHAIR No. 1305

LIBRARY TABLE No. 410-L
30″ high, 48″ hexagon top

ARM CHAIR No. 2616

PLANT STAND No. 52-T
22″ high, top 17″ x 17″

PLANT STAND No. 53-T
22″ high, top 17″ x 17″

TABLE No. 436
28″ high, top 24″ diameter

LIBRARY TABLE No. 446
30″ high, 48″ diameter

ADJUSTABLE-BACK CHAIR No. 2342

DINING CHAIR No. 1300

EXTENSION TABLE No. 934-E
30″ high, top 54″ and 60″ diameter
Made to extend to 10 and 12 feet

"EASTWOOD" ARM CHAIR No. 2638

37" high, 34" wide, 33" deep

TABLE No. 449

22" high, top 24" diameter

SMOKER'S CABINET No. 522

27" high, 17" wide, 15" deep

ARM CHAIR No. 2590

LIBRARY TABLE No. 461

30" high, 32" wide, 54" long
Drawer Pulls of wrought iron or copper

ARM ROCKER No. 2603
ARM CHAIR No. 2604

PLANT STAND No. 41

28" high, top 14" x 14"

STOOL No. 729

15" high, 16" wide, 20" long

ADJUSTABLE-BACK CHAIR No. 2340

WRITING DESK No. 550

48″ high, 33″ wide, 14″ deep
Hinges and Pulls of wrought iron or copper

WRITING TABLE No. 459

29″ high, 42″ long, 24″ wide
Draw Pulls of wrought iron or copper

SCREEN No. 102

65″ high, 3 panels 48″ wide

DINING CHAIR No. 1296
ARM CHAIR No. 1296-A

DINING TABLE No. 935

30″ high, 48″ wide, 96″ long

SCREEN No. 111

58″ high, 3 panels 54″ wide

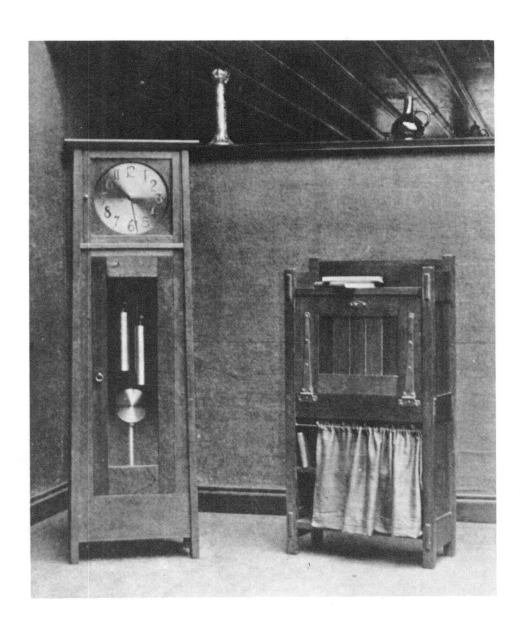

HALL CLOCK No. 3

72″ high, 21″ wide, 14″ deep

WRITING DESK No. 518

51″ high, 26″ wide, 11″ deep
Hinges and Key Plate wrought iron or copper

FIRE SCREEN No. 104
33″ high, 31″ wide

CARD TABLE No. 447
29″ high, 18″ wide, 30″ long
Drawer in each end

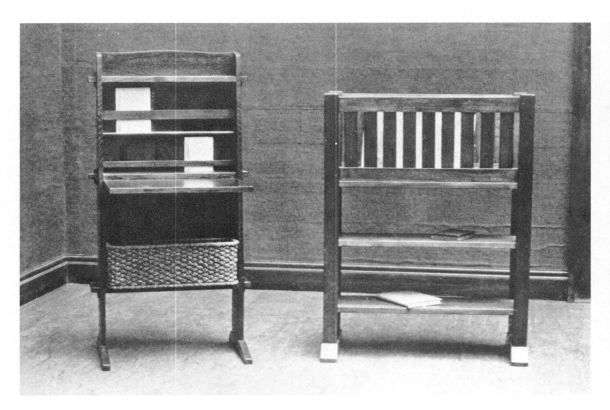

WRITING DESK No. 505
46″ high, 22″ wide, 7″ deep
Waste paper basket in Rush

PAPER RACK No. 551
40″ high, 30″ long, 13″ wide

BOOK CASE No. 542
 56″ high, 36″ wide, 12″ deep
 Metal of wrought iron or copper
 Plain Glass

BOOK SHELVES No. 532
 56″ high, 36″ wide, 12″ deep

BOOK CASE No. 544
 56″ high, 62″ wide, 12″ deep
 Metal of wrought iron or copper
 Plain Glass

CHEST. CEDAR LINED

25″ high, 41″ long, 20″ wide.
Mountings of wrought iron.

PIANO BENCH No. 175
21″ high, top 15″ x 36″

TRUNK REST No. 552
16″ high, 18″ wide, 34″ long

MAGAZINE CABINET No. 547

35″ high, top 16″ x 16″
4 shelves

ALSO MAGAZINE CABINET No. 548

44″ high, top 16″ x 16″
5 shelves

COSTUMER No. 192

60″ high, 14″ wide
Hooks of wrought iron

BEDSTEAD No. 600

Foot 30", head 46" high
58" wide, 80" long

BEDSTEAD No. 620

Foot 30" high, Head 46" high
58" wide, 80" long

MIRROR No. 607
20″ wide, 34″ long
Plain Glass

MIRROR No. 608
26″ high, 36″ long
Plain Glass

HALL MIRROR No. 609
28″ high, 48″ long
Plain Glass
Hooks in wrought iron

SOMNO No. 618

34″ high, 20″ wide, 16″ deep

CHEVAL GLASS No. 35

70″ high, 34″ wide
Plain Mirror 22″ x 54″

WASHSTAND No. 628

29″ high, 40″ long, 21″ deep

DRESSER No. 625

33″ high, 42″ long, 22″ deep
Plain Mirror 24″ x 34″

CHEST OF DRAWERS No. 626

40″ high, 36″ wide, 20″ deep

CHEST OF DRAWERS No. 627

50″ high, 40″ wide, 22″ deep

CHEST OF DRAWERS No. 614

62″ high, 42″ wide, 22″ deep
Hinges and Pulls of wrought iron or copper

WARDROBE No. 624

72″ high, 32″ wide, 21″ deep
Plain Mirror 19″ x 47″

CHEST OF DRAWERS No. 622
50″ high, 40″ wide, 22″ deep
Drawer Pulls of wrought iron or copper

CHEST OF DRAWERS No. 621
40″ high, 36″ wide, 20″ deep
Drawer Pulls of wrought iron or copper

Drawer Pulls and Candlesticks of wrought
   iron or copper
Plain Mirror 20″ x 40″

DRESSING TABLE No. 632
30″ high, 54″ long, 22″ deep
57″ to top of mirror

DRESSER No. 616

33" high, 54" long, 22" deep
Metal in wrought iron or copper

MIRROR No. 633

30" high, 54" long
Metal in wrought iron or copper
Plain Glass, 24" x 48"

SIDE CHAIR No. 1295
ARM CHAIR No. 1295-A

CORNER CABINET No. 972
70" high, 47" wide
Metal of wrought iron or copper

HALL SEAT No. 172
33" high, 56" long, 20" deep

CHINA CABINET No. 964

69″ high, 42″ wide, 16″ deep
Metal in wrought iron or copper
Plain or Leaded Glass

SIDEBOARD No. 971

   36″ high, 54″ long, 23″ deep
   Draw and Door Pulls wrought iron or copper

DINING CHAIR No. 1304
ARM CHAIR No. 1304-A

SERVING TABLE No. 970

   36″ high, 20″ wide, 48″ long
   Drawer Pulls of wrought iron or copper

DINING CHAIR No. 1301
ARM CHAIR No. 1301-A

SIDEBOARD No. 967

39″ high, 60″ long, 24″ wide
Metal of wrought iron or copper

WINE COOLER No. 553

15″ high, top 13″, bottom 14″ diameter
Hoops and handles of wrought iron or copper

SERVING TABLE No. 962½

Same as above.   40″ long, 2 drawers

SERVING TABLE No. 962

36″ high, 60″ long, 17″ deep

Drawer Pulls of wrought iron or copper

BUFFET No. 955

38" high, 60" long, 24" deep

DINING CHAIR No. 1301

SIDEBOARD No. 961

50" high, 70" long. 25" deep

Hinges and Pulls of wrought iron or copper

SCREEN No. 110

Three-Panel, each 17″ wide, 58″ high

SIDE CHAIR No. 1303
ARM CHAIR No. 1303-A

DINNER GONG

37″ high, 24″ wide
Gong 18″ diameter

EXTENSION TABLE No. 969-E

30″ high, top 48″, 54″ and 60″ diameter
Made to extend 10 and 12 feet

DINING CHAIR No. 1297
ARM CHAIR No. 1297-A

ARM CHAIR No. 2639

TABLE No. 441
30" high, top 36" diameter

OFFICE CHAIR No. 2639½

TABLE No. 439
26" high, top 26" diameter

ROLL TOP DESK No. 457 R. T.
44″ high, 32″ wide, 60″ long
Metal in wrought iron or copper

CABINET TOP DESK No. 457-C
36″ high, 32″ wide, 60″ long
Metal in wrought iron or copper

Inlaid Oak Fall Front Desk, designed by Harvey Ellis and executed by Gustav Stickley

THE CRAFTSMAN WORKSHOPS SYRACUSE, N. Y.

Supplement to Catalogue D.

INTRODUCTION

THIS catalogue is issued merely as a supplement to our Furniture Catalogue D, which contains descriptions, illustrations and prices of the bulk of the cabinet work produced in THE CRAFTSMAN WORKSHOPS. The pieces shown in this book are from new designs which have been made since the publication of the main furniture catalogue. Most of them are in the well-known CRAFTSMAN style, simple, massive, roomy pieces of furniture, designed for comfort, and so solidly built that they will last for generations,—the furniture that has made a name and a place for itself too prominent to need further description. Two new departures have been made, however, among these later products of THE CRAFTSMAN WORKSHOPS, and both are in the direction of somewhat lighter, although just as reliable, construction. Some of the pieces are built after our familiar models, but on rather lighter lines, so that they are easier to handle and also are somewhat less expensive. These pieces are as handsome and as durable as the more massive furniture, but are suited to smaller rooms. The new pieces differ in form from the broad, low, solid models that have hitherto charac-

terized all the CRAFTSMAN furniture. They are built on more slender lines, tall, graceful, and showing an effect of quaint refinement. The use of light spindles instead of the broad bars in the backs of chairs and settles gives an effect that is rather more ornate than that of the heavier pieces, although it is in reality quite as structural and simple. The wood used in all the new pieces is the famous CRAFTSMAN Fumed Oak, and the accessories of CRAFTSMAN Canvas, CRAFTSMAN Hard or Soft Leather, or CRAFTSMAN Sheepskin, used as seat covers, cushions, etc., are the same as described in Furniture Catalogue D. All the metal-work, such as locks, keys, pulls, and escutcheons, is hand-wrought in THE CRAFTSMAN WORKSHOPS, and is of the brass or copper which shows the richness of color obtained by our peculiar process of firing, or of iron in our soft "armor-bright" finish. Another novelty shown in this supplement is a group of pieces for the use of children, so built that they will give delight to generation after generation of little ones. Some of the sturdy little chairs and tables are shown in Catalogue D, but we illustrate here additional pieces enough to completely furnish a child's room.

SETTLE   NUMBER 219

Made in Craftsman Fumed Oak or Mahogany, 38″ high, 72″ long, 24″ deep.
Seat cushion covered with Craftsman Canvas, Sheepskin or Soft Leather.

CRAFTSMAN CANVAS		SHEEPSKIN		SOFT LEATHER	
Oak,	$32.00	Oak,	$37.50	Oak,	$41.50
Mahogany,	41.25	Mahogany,	46.75	Mahogany,	51.75

SETTLE   NUMBER 212

Made in Craftsman Fumed Oak or Mahogany, 36″ high, 48″ long, 22″ deep.
Seat covered with Craftsman Canvas, Sheepskin or Soft Leather, ornamental
nails of dull brass.

CRAFTSMAN CANVAS		SHEEPSKIN		SOFT LEATHER	
Oak,	$18.00	Oak,	$21.00	Oak,	$24.00
Mahogany,	23.25	Mahogany,	26.25	Mahogany,	29.50

S E T T L E   NUMBER 221

Made in Craftsman Fumed Oak, 76″ long, 39″ high, 29″ deep.   Seat cushion
covered with Craftsman Canvas, Sheepskin or Soft Leather.

Craftsman Canvas,   . $55.00   Sheepskin,   .   . $69.00
Soft Leather,   .   .   75.00

S E T T L E   NUMBER 218

Made in Craftsman Fumed Oak or Mahogany, 38″ high, 48″ long, 22″ deep.
Seat cushion covered with Craftsman Canvas, Sheepskin or Soft Leather.

CRAFTSMAN CANVAS		SHEEPSKIN		SOFT LEATHER	
Oak, .	$29.00	Oak, .	$32.00	Oak, .	$35.00
Mahogany, .	37.00	Mahogany, .	40.00	Mahogany, .	43.00

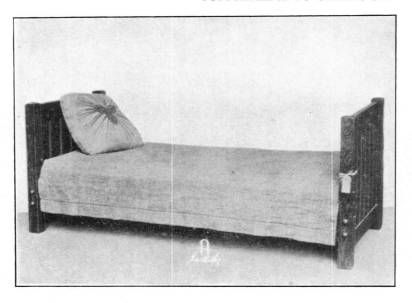

COUCH   BED   NUMBER 220

Made in Craftsman Fumed Oak, 34″ high, 84″ long, 36″ deep.   Provided
with Floss Mattress and Box Spring.

Price, Complete with Floss Mattress and Box Spring,   .   . $50.00
 "   Craftsman Canvas Spread Embroidered,   .   .   .   8.00

REVOLVING   BOOK   RACK   NUMBER 90

Made in Craftsman Fumed Oak, 12″ square.   Price,   . $4.00

RECLINING   CHAIR   NUMBER 346

Made in Craftsman Fumed Oak or Mahogany. Seat and back cushions
covered with Craftsman Canvas, Sheepskin or Soft Leather.
Height of back, 36″.   Height of seat, 17″.   Size of seat, 21″ wide, 24″ deep.

CRAFTSMAN CANVAS		SHEEPSKIN		SOFT LEATHER	
Oak, .	$22.50	Oak, .	$26.00	Oak, .	$31.00
Mahogany, .	26.00	Mahogany, .	29.50	Mahogany, .	34.50

SETTLE   NUMBER 286
(Patented August 8, 1905).
Made in Craftsman Fumed Oak or Mahogany, 49″ high, 48″ long, 20″ deep.
Seat in Rush or Soft Leather.
Oak, $27.00   Mahogany, $34.00

CHAIR   NUMBER 384
(Patented August 8, 1905).
Made in Craftsman Fumed Oak or Mahogany.   Seat in Rush or Soft Leather.
Height of back from floor, 46″.   Height of seat from floor, 18″.   Size of seat,
19″ wide, 17″ deep.
Oak,   .   .   . $10.00   Mahogany,   .   . $13.00
ARM   CHAIR (To Match)   NUMBER 386
Oak,   .   .   . $13.50   Mahogany,   .   . $17.00

R O C K E R   (Patented August 8, 1905).   NUMBER 377
Made in Craftsman Fumed Oak or Mahogany. Slip seat in Rush or Soft Leather.
Height of back from floor, 36″. Height of seat from floor, 14″. Size of seat,
16″ wide, 14″ deep.
Oak,   .   .   . $7.00   Mahogany,   .   . $9.00
C H A I R (To Match)   NUMBER 378
Oak,   .   .   . $7.00   Mahogany,   .   . $9.00

L I B R A R Y   T A B L E   NUMBER 655
Made in Craftsman Fumed Oak or Mahogany, 29″ high, 36″ long, 24″ wide.
Oak, Wood Top,   . $14.00   Mahogany,   .   . $17.00
Number 657. Size—29″ high, 48″ long, 30″ wide. Same construction as No.
655 Table.
Oak, Wood Top,   . $21.00   Mahogany,   .   . $27.00

ARM ROCKER   NUMBER 375
               (Patented August 8, 1905).

CRAFTSMAN CANVAS	SHEEPSKIN	SOFT LEATHER
Oak, . $17.50	Oak, . $18.50	Oak, . $19.50
Mahogany, . 21.75	Mahogany, . 22.75	Mahogany, . 23.75

ARM CHAIR (To Match) Same Prices   NUMBER 376

ROCKER   NUMBER 373
               (Patented August 8, 1905).

CRAFTSMAN CANVAS	SHEEPSKIN	SOFT LEATHER
Oak, . $9.75	Oak, . $10.75	Oak, . $11.75
Mahogany, . 12.25	Mahogany, . 13.25	Mahogany, . 14.25

CHAIR   (To Match) Same Prices   NUMBER 374

R E C L I N I N G   C H A I R   Number 368
(Patented August 8, 1905).

Made in Craftsman Fumed Oak or Mahogany, Swing seat of heavy brown duck stretched across frame affording firm but elastic support to seat cushion.   Height of back from floor, 36'' Height of seat from floor, 15''   Size of seat 21'', between arms, 26'' deep

CRAFTSMAN CANVAS		SHEEPSKIN		SOFT LEATHER	
Oak,	$25.50	Oak,	$32.00	Oak,	$37.00
Mahogany,	31.50	Mahogany,	38.00	Mahogany,	43.00

R E C L I N I N G   C H A I R   Number 367
(Patented August 8, 1905).

Made of Craftsman Fumed Oak or Mahogany. Swing seat of heavy brown duck stretched across frame, affording firm but elastic support to seat cushion. Height of back from floor, 36''.   Height of seat from floor, 15''.   Size of seat 19'' between arms, 24'' deep.

CRAFTSMAN CANVAS		SHEEPSKIN		SOFT LEATHER	
Oak,	$24.00	Oak,	$29.00	Oak,	$34.00
Mahogany,	29.00	Mahogany,	34.00	Mahogany,	39.00

R E C L I N I N G   C H A I R   NUMBER 369
(Patented August 8, 1905).
Same construction as 367–368.

CRAFTSMAN CANVAS		SHEEPSKIN		SOFT LEATHER	
Oak,	. $27.50	Oak,	. $34.50	Oak,	. $40.00
Mahogany,	. 34.50	Mahogany,	. 41.50	Mahogany,	. 47.00

A R M   R O C K E R   NUMBER 365
Made in Craftsman Fumed Oak.   Seat covered with Sheepskin or Soft Leather.
Height of back from floor, 38″.   Height of seat, 15″.   Size of seat, 22″ wide
between arms, 20″ deep.
Sheepskin,   .   . $8.50   Soft Leather,   .   .   10.00

A R M   C H A I R   (To Match)   NUMBER 366
Sheepskin,   .   . $8.50   Soft Leather,.   .   .   10.00

A R M   R O C K E R   Number 381

Made of Craftsman Fumed Oak.   Swing seat and back made of hard leather·
Height of back from floor, 39″.   Height of seat from floor, 15″.   Size of seat,
18″ between arms, 18″ deep.

Price, ... $10.00

A R M   C H A I R   (To Match)   Number 382

Price, ... $10.00

S M A L L   R O C K E R   Number 379

Same construction as above.

Price, ... $7.00

S M A L L   C H A I R   Number 380

Price, ... $7.00

S I D E B O A R D   NUMBER 817

Made in Craftsman Fumed Oak with hand-wrought iron hinges, pulls and knobs, 50″ high, 70″ wide, 25″ deep.

Price, ... $84.00

S I D E B O A R D   Number 816

Made in Craftsman Fumed Oak, with hand-wrought iron or copper locks and pulls, 46″ high, 48″ wide, 18″ deep.   Suitable for a small dining room.

Price, ... $30,50

D I N I N G   C H A I R   NUMBER 370
Made in Fumed Oak or Mahogany.   Slip seat in Rush or Soft Leather.
Height of back from floor, 36″.   Height of seat from floor, 18″.   Size of seat,
17″ wide, 16″ deep.   Oak,   . $6.25   Mahogany,   .   8.00
A R M   D I N I N G   C H A I R (To Match)   NUMBER 370A
Oak,   .   .   . $10.75   Mahogany,   .   . $13.75

D I N I N G   T A B L E   NUMBER 656
Made in Craftsman Fumed Oak or Mahogany, with extension top.

OAK		MAHOGANY	
54″ top to extend 10 ft.,	. $62.00	54″ top to extend 10 ft.,	. $77.00
54″ top to extend 12 ft.,	. 72.00	54″ top to extend 12 ft.,	. 90.00
60″ top to extend 12 ft.,	. 85.00	60″ top to extend 12 ft.,	. 100.00

C E L L A R E T T E   NUMBER 86

Made in Craftsman Fumed Oak, 43" high, 24" wide, 17" deep. Top and upper shelf covered with copper. Small inside cabinet for cigars has flat key lock. Hand-wrought iron or copper pulls and lock.

Price, ... $30.00

C E L L A R E T T E   NUMBER 88

Made in Craftsman Fumed Oak, 35" high, 18" wide, 18" deep, with top open, 18" x 36". Has top opening out in two leaves from center, which is covered with copper. Hand-wrought iron or copper pulls and lock.

Price, ... $22.50

CELLARETTE   NUMBER 87

Made in Craftsman Fumed Oak, 40″ high, 22″ wide, 16″ deep. Sliding shelf covered with copper. Hand-wrought iron or copper pulls and lock.

Price, ... $25.00

SMOKER'S CABINET   NUMBER 89

Made in Craftsman Fumed Oak, 29″ high, 20″ wide, 15″ deep. Conveniently arranged shelves and compartments for bottles, cigar boxes and tobacco jars. Hand-wrought iron or copper pulls and lock.

Price, ... $12.00

D E S K   NUMBER 729

Made in Craftsman Fumed Oak, 43″ high, 36″ wide, 14″ deep. Pulls and
fittings of wrought iron or copper.

Price, $36.00

D E S K   NUMBER 729

Made in Craftsman Fumed Oak, 43″ high, 36″ wide, 14″ deep. Pulls and
fittings of wrought iron or copper.

Price, $36.00

D E S K   NUMBER 728

Made in Craftsman Fumed Oak, 39″ high, 30″ wide, 14″ deep.

Price, $16.00

D E S K   NUMBER 728

Made in Craftsman Fumed Oak, 39″ high, 30″ wide, 14″ deep.

Price, ... $16.00

LIBRARY TABLE   NUMBER 652

Made in Craftsman Fumed Oak, 29″ high, 36″ long, 24″ wide.   Pulls in hand-
wrought iron or copper.

Wood Top,   .   . $13.50   Hard Leather Top,   . $22,50

LIBRARY TABLE   NUMBER 653

Made in Craftsman Fumed Oak, 29″ high, 48″ long, 30″ wide.
Wood Top,   .   . $20.00   Hard Leather Top,   . $34.00

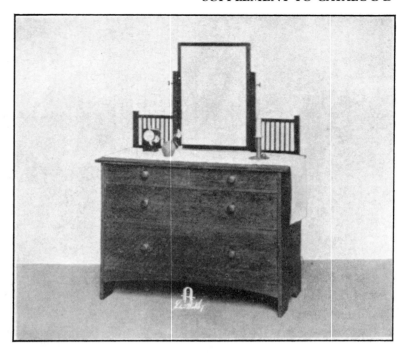

CHILD'S DRESSER   NUMBER 921

Made in Craftsman Fumed Oak, 40″ high, 26″ wide, 16″ deep; mirror, 14″ x 20″.   Just the right height and size for a child's room.

Price, ... $18.00

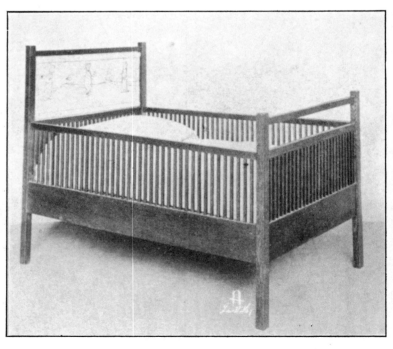

CHILD'S BED   NUMBER 919

Made in Craftsman Fumed Oak, 33″ wide, 52″ long, (inside measurements). Head, 43″ high, foot, 34″ high.

Price,   .   .   .   , ... $16.00

CHILD'S WARDROBE   NUMBER 920

Made in Craftsman Fumed Oak, 60″ high, 33″ wide, 16″ deep. Compart-ments for hats, shoes and toys; shallow trays for little suits and dresses.

Price, ... $30.00

CHILD'S WARDROBE   NUMBER 920

Made in Craftsman Fumed Oak, 60″ high, 33″ wide, 16″ deep. Compart-ments for hats, shoes and toys; shallow trays for little suits and dresses.

Price, ... $30.00

CHILD'S TABLE NUMBER 640

Made in Craftsman Fumed Oak or Silver Gray Maple, 18″ high, 28″ long, 20″ wide. To match in size the Child's Chairs shown in Furniture Catalogue D.

Oak, ... $3.50   Maple, . . . $4.50

CHILD'S HIGH CHAIR NUMBER 388

Made in Craftsman Fumed Oak with Rush seat. Adjustable tray that lifts over the back.

Height of back from floor, 38″. Height of seat from floor, 24″. Size of seat, 12″ between arms, 12″ deep.

Price, ... $12.00

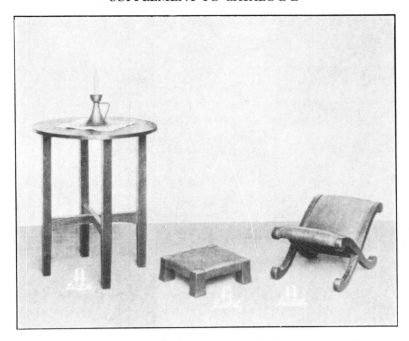

R O U N D   T A B L E   NUMBER 654

Made in Craftsman Fumed Oak or Mahogany, 29″ high, 24″ diameter.

Oak, Wood Top, . $6.25   Mahogany, . 8.00
Hard Leather Top, . 10.75

S T O O L   NUMBER 302

Made in Craftsman Fumed Oak or Mahogany, 5″ high, 12″ square.

CRAFTSMAN CANVAS		SHEEPSKIN		SOFT LEATHER	
Oak, .	$2.25	Oak, .	$2.50	Oak, .	$2.75
Mahogany, .	2.75	Mahogany, .	3.00	Mahogany, .	3.25

F O O T   S T O O L   NUMBER 389

Made in Craftsman Fumed Oak or Mahogany.

CRAFTSMAN CANVAS		SHEEPSKIN		SOFT LEATHER	
Oak, .	$4.50	Oak, .	$5.50	Oak, .	$6.50
Mahogany, .	6.50	Mahogany, .	7.00	Mahogany, .	8.00

T H E   C R A F T S M A N   D E V I C E S

EVERY piece of furniture produced from **THE CRAFTS-MAN WORKSHOPS** shows **THE CRAFTSMAN** device, the joiner's compass enclosing our motto, "ALS IK KAN," stamped in red in some unobtrusive place, and also bears **THE CRAFTSMAN LEATHER TAG**, attached by raffia in such a position that it may be plainly seen as a guarantee of authenticity.

Inlaid Oak Music Cabinet, designed by Harvey Ellis and executed by Gustav Stickley

CRAFTSMAN WILLOW FURNITURE

The Craftman, September 1906

WILLOW FURNITURE: The right kind of willow furniture affords exactly the relief that is necessary to lighten the general effect of the darker and heavier oak pieces of Craftsman furniture. Our willow pieces, while strongly and firmly made, have yet the flexibility of a well woven basket. They are finished usually in soft green, deep golden brown, light golden brown, straw and natural color, although they may also be had in soft blue, gray and mahogany, if desired. In each case the color is more or less uneven, varying as it might in the growing willow.

The cushions are covered with our Craftsman canvas, flamme, Pompeian cloth and velour in tones to match the willow, also hand printed linens and cretonnes of our own designs and colorings. The prices quoted include cushions in any of the above materials except velour, which is somewhat more expensive. Samples of all our coverings will be sent on application.

Some of our latest models are shown on pages 50, 51 and 52. In addition to these we have many lower-priced willow pieces, descriptions of which will be given upon request.

92

No. 92
WILLOW CHAIR $26.00
BACK 32 IN. HIGH. ARMS 32 IN. HIGH. SEAT 15 IN. HIGH, 23½ IN. WIDE, 24 IN. DEEP

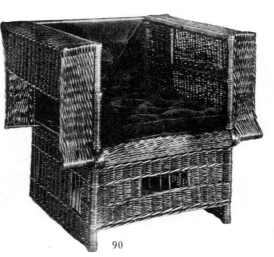

90

No. 90
WILLOW CHAIR . $27.50
BACK 29½ IN. HIGH
ARMS 29½ IN. HIGH
SEAT 14½ IN. HIGH, 22 IN. WIDE, 24 IN. DEEP

91

No. 91
WILLOW CHAIR . $25.00
BACK 39 IN. HIGH
ARMS 24¾ IN. HIGH
SEAT 14 IN. HIGH, 21½ IN. WIDE, 24 IN. DEEP

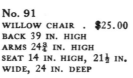

TRADE-MARK REG'D   IN U.S. PATENT OFFICE

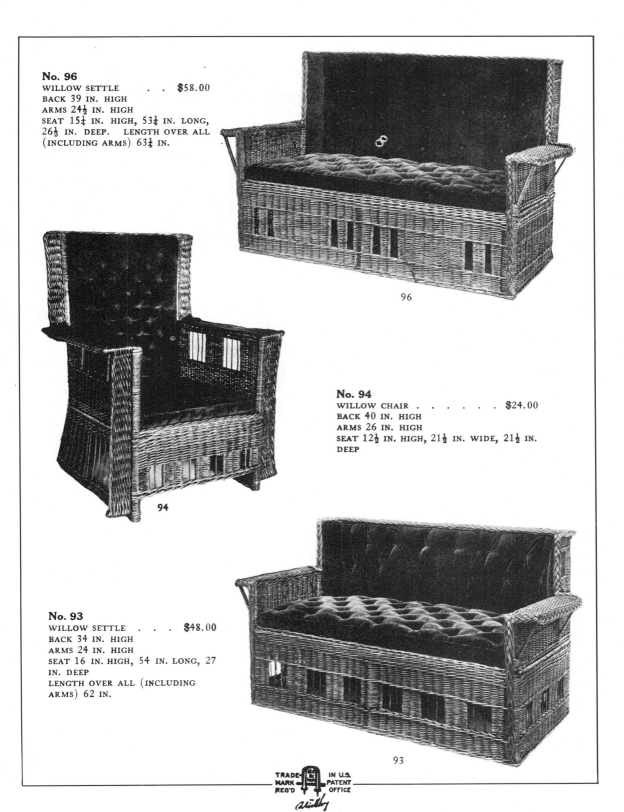

No. 96
WILLOW SETTLE . . $58.00
BACK 39 IN. HIGH
ARMS 24½ IN. HIGH
SEAT 15¼ IN. HIGH, 53¼ IN. LONG,
26½ IN. DEEP.   LENGTH OVER ALL
(INCLUDING ARMS) 63¼ IN.

96

No. 94
WILLOW CHAIR $24.00
BACK 40 IN. HIGH
ARMS 26 IN. HIGH
SEAT 12½ IN. HIGH, 21½ IN. WIDE, 21½ IN.
DEEP

94

No. 93
WILLOW SETTLE . . . $48.00
BACK 34 IN. HIGH
ARMS 24 IN. HIGH
SEAT 16 IN. HIGH, 54 IN. LONG, 27
IN. DEEP
LENGTH OVER ALL (INCLUDING
ARMS) 62 IN.

93

TRADE MARK REG'D — IN U.S. PATENT OFFICE

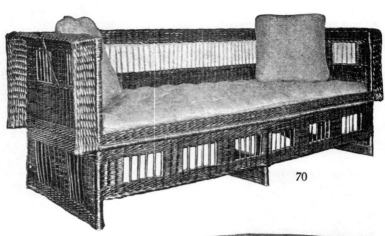

No. 70

WILLOW SETTLE . $68.00
INCLUDING TWO PILLOWS.
BACK 32 IN. HIGH. SEAT
17 IN. HIGH, 78 IN. LONG,
27 IN. DEEP. LENGTH
OVER ALL 86 IN.

70

No. 56

WILLOW CHAIR $20.00
ARMS 31 IN. HIGH. SEAT 17 IN. HIGH, 22 IN.
WIDE, 23 IN. DEEP.

56

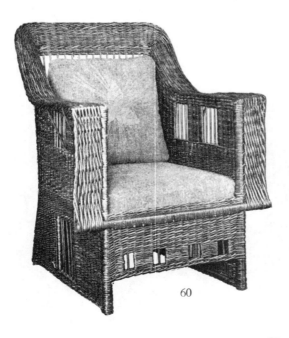

No. 60

WILLOW CHAIR $24.50
BACK 39 IN. HIGH. ARMS 30 IN. HIGH.
SEAT 17 IN. HIGH, 22 IN. WIDE, 23 IN. DEEP.

60

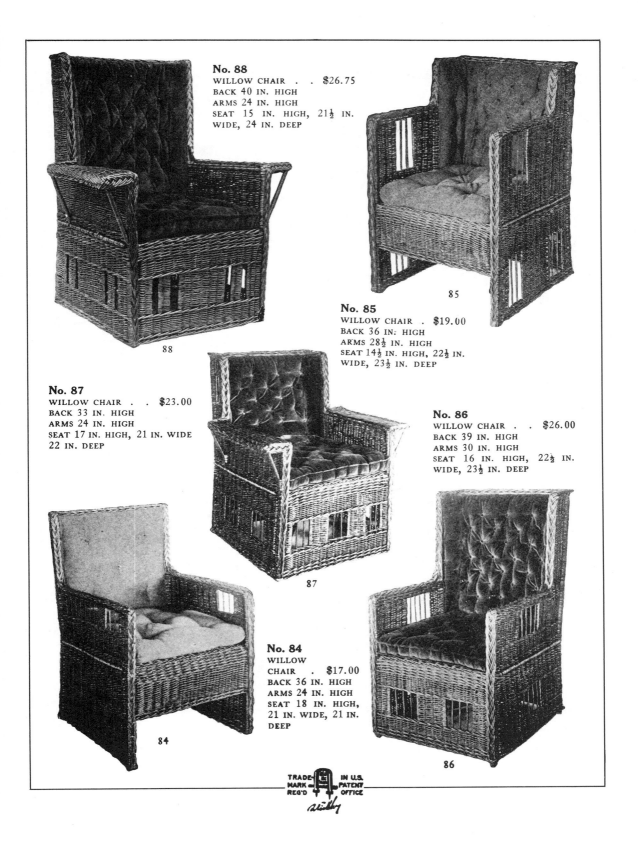

No. 88
WILLOW CHAIR . . $26.75
BACK 40 IN. HIGH
ARMS 24 IN. HIGH
SEAT 15 IN. HIGH, 21½ IN.
WIDE, 24 IN. DEEP

85

No. 85
WILLOW CHAIR . $19.00
BACK 36 IN. HIGH
ARMS 28½ IN. HIGH
SEAT 14½ IN. HIGH, 22½ IN.
WIDE, 23½ IN. DEEP

88

No. 87
WILLOW CHAIR . . $23.00
BACK 33 IN. HIGH
ARMS 24 IN. HIGH
SEAT 17 IN. HIGH, 21 IN. WIDE
22 IN. DEEP

No. 86
WILLOW CHAIR . . $26.00
BACK 39 IN. HIGH
ARMS 30 IN. HIGH
SEAT 16 IN. HIGH, 22½ IN.
WIDE, 23½ IN. DEEP

87

No. 84
WILLOW
CHAIR . $17.00
BACK 36 IN. HIGH
ARMS 24 IN. HIGH
SEAT 18 IN. HIGH,
21 IN. WIDE, 21 IN.
DEEP

84

86

TRADE- IN U.S.
MARK PATENT
REG'D OFFICE

143

No. 500
WILLOW CHAIR . . . $10.50
BACK 34 IN. HIGH. ARMS 21¾ IN. HIGH. SEAT 17 IN. HIGH, 17 IN. WIDE, 18 IN. DEEP.

No. 35
WILLOW CHAIR $8.75
BACK 34 IN. HIGH. SEAT 17 IN. HIGH, 17 IN. WIDE, 17 IN. DEEP.

No. 68
WILLOW ROCKER . . . $9.00
BACK 34 IN. HIGH, ARMS 24½ IN. HIGH, SEAT 17 IN. HIGH, 20 IN. WIDE, 20 IN. DEEP.

No. 68½
WILLOW CHAIR $8.75
SAME DIMENSIONS AS NO. 68.

No. 523½
WILLOW ROCKER $7.25
SAME DIMENSIONS AS NO. 523.

35

523

No. 523
WILLOW CHAIR $7.00
BACK 33 IN. HIGH. ARMS 23 IN. HIGH. SEAT 17 IN. HIGH, 17½ IN. WIDE, 18 IN. DEEP.

68

TRADE-MARK REG'D IN U.S. PATENT OFFICE

No. 72

WILLOW SETTLE . . . $43.00
BACK 33 IN. HIGH. ARMS 28
IN. HIGH. SEAT 17 IN. HIGH.
54 IN. LONG, 26 IN. DEEP.
LENGTH OVER ALL 66 IN.

72

No. 68

WILLOW CHAIR $10.00
BACK 37 IN. HIGH. ARMS 24½ IN. HIGH. SEAT
17 IN. HIGH, 21 IN. WIDE, 20 IN. DEEP

68

No. 54½

WILLOW CHAIR $14.00
BACK 33 IN. HIGH. ARMS 29 IN. HIGH.
SEAT 17 IN. HIGH, 20 IN. WIDE, 19 IN. DEEP.

FOR MORE WILLOW CHAIRS
SEE PAGE 62.

54½

TRADE IN U.S.
MARK PATENT
REG'D OFFICE

No. 52
WILLOW CHAIR $15.00
BACK 38 IN. HIGH. ARMS 26 IN. HIGH.
SEAT 17 IN. HIGH, 21 IN. WIDE, 20 IN. DEEP.

No. 51
WILLOW ROCKER $15.00
SAME DESIGN AND DIMENSIONS AS 52.

52

58

No. 58
WILLOW CHAIR $17.00
BACK 37 IN. HIGH. ARMS 24 IN. HIGH. SEAT
15 IN. HIGH, 21 IN. WIDE, 19 IN. DEEP.

No. 59
WILLOW ROCKER $17.00
SAME DESIGN AND DIMENSIONS AS 58.

64

No. 64
WILLOW CHAIR $22.50
BACK 33 IN. HIGH. ARMS 28 IN. HIGH.
SEAT 17 IN. HIGH, 21 IN. WIDE, 23 IN. DEEP.

61

No. 61
WILLOW ROCKER $10.50
BACK 33 IN. HIGH.   ARMS 24 IN. HIGH.   SEAT 16 IN.
HIGH, 17 IN. WIDE, 18 IN. DEEP.

No. 50
WILLOW CHAIR $15.00
BACK 34 IN. HIGH.   ARMS 24 IN. HIGH.   SEAT 15 IN.
HIGH, 21 IN. WIDE, 19 IN. DEEP.

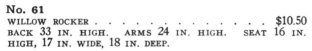

601

No. 601. Electric light with shade; canopy made in hammered copper, brass or wrought iron, and chain of wrought iron; supplied with chain socket; sweet grass shade, 9 in. in diameter and 4 in. high. Price, $3.00.

No. 66
WILLOW STOOL $7.50
17 IN. HIGH.   SEAT 20 IN. SQUARE.

50

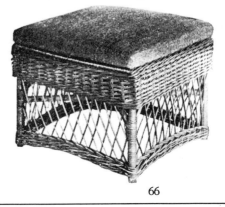

66

Copper and Glass Chandelier from the Craftsman Workshops

CRAFTSMAN LAMPS AND HANGING FIXTURES

The Craftman, July 1906

LIGHTING FIXTURES: The lighting fixtures shown here are made in iron, copper and brass, the metal selected depending on the design of the piece and the decorative scheme in which it is to be used. The wrought iron is finished in a way known in England as "armor bright." This is an old finishing process used by English metal workers, which prevents the surface from rusting and brings out all the black, gray and silvery tones natural to iron. The lamp shades and domes can be obtained with either amber, straw-colored or crystal glass.

One of the most distinctive features of our lighting fixtures is the willow shades. These are made for us in Japan from Craftsman models. They are firmly woven and lined with a heavy grade of Habutai silk in soft shades of green, red, dull yellow and orange. The combination of materials is as harmonious and restful as it is effective, allowing a maximum of mellow light to be diffused into the room through the colored silk between the fine willow strands. For prices of separate shades see page 8.

SHADE B

SHADE A   55

50

No. 50
THREE-LIGHT ELECTRIC LAMP $18.50 HAMMERED COPPER FURNISHED WITH SHADE A OR B. 21 IN. HIGH OVER ALL. BASE 7 IN. IN DIAMETER. SHADE 18 IN. IN DIAMETER, 9 IN. HIGH.

No. 55
ONE-LIGHT ELECTRIC LAMP . . . . $4.35 FURNISHED WITH SHADE A OR B. FUMED OAK STANDARD 9 IN. HIGH. 14 IN. HIGH OVER ALL. BASE 8 IN. IN DIAMETER. SHADE 10 IN. IN DIAMETER, 5 IN. HIGH.

53

502

No. 53
WOODEN CANDLESTICK $3.00 FITTED WITH GLASS CONTAINER FOR FLAT CANDLE. STAINED IN MAHOGANY OR ANY OF OUR REGULAR OAK FINISHES. STANDARD 10 IN. HIGH. 15 IN. HIGH OVER ALL. JAPANESE SPLIT BAMBOO SHADE 10 IN. IN DIAMETER, 5 IN. HIGH.

No. 502
ONE-LIGHT ELECTRIC LAMP WITH GLASS SHADE . . $15.00 WITH JAPANESE WICKER SHADE $9.00 FUMED OAK STANDARD BANDED WITH HAMMERED COPPER AT TOP AND BOTTOM. 17 IN. HIGH OVER ALL. BASE 7 IN. SQUARE THE SHADE IS MADE OF SMALL LIGHTS OF OPALESCENT GLASS SET IN COPPER.

TRADE-MARK REG'D IN U.S. PATENT OFFICE

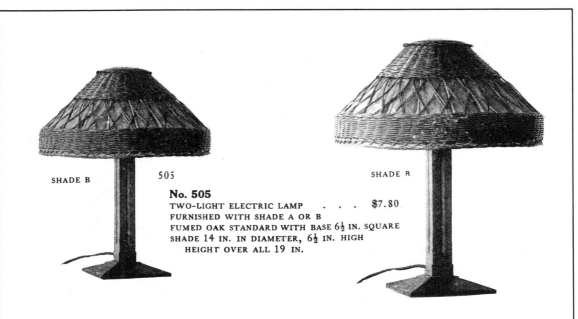

SHADE B   505   SHADE B

No. 505

TWO-LIGHT ELECTRIC LAMP . . . $7.80
FURNISHED WITH SHADE A OR B
FUMED OAK STANDARD WITH BASE 6½ IN. SQUARE
SHADE 14 IN. IN DIAMETER, 6½ IN. HIGH
    HEIGHT OVER ALL 19 IN.

No. 50

THREE-LIGHT ELECTRIC LAMP . . . $18.50
HAMMERED COPPER.   21 IN. HIGH OVER ALL
BASE 7 IN. IN DIAMETER
WICKER SHADE 18 IN. IN DIAMETER, 7 IN. HIGH
LINED WITH FIGURED OR PLAIN SILK IN BROWN
RED, GREEN OR YELLOW

No. 507

THREE-LIGHT ELECTRIC LAMP . . . $12.00
FURNISHED WITH SHADE A OR B
FUMED OAK STANDARD WITH BASE 7¾ IN. SQUARE
SHADE 18 IN. IN DIAMETER, 8 IN. HIGH
HEIGHT OVER ALL 22 IN.

50

SHADE B

No. 57

ONE-LIGHT ELECTRIC LAMP . . . $5.75
FURNISHED WITH SHADE A OR B
POTTERY STANDARD 9½ IN. HIGH
14½ IN. HIGH OVER ALL
BASE 5 IN. IN DIAMETER
SHADE 10 IN. IN DIAMETER, 5 IN. HIGH

57

No. 376. Oil lamp, fount of hammered copper in frame of wrought iron; shade, No. 668, of copper cut out in stencil design and lined with fine brass wire cloth over a foundation of cream linen, fringe of tiny brass chains; height to top of burner, 15 in. Diameter of shade at bottom, 15 in. Price of lamp with shade complete, $22.00; price of shade, $10.00.

No. 625. Electric lamp in fumed oak and hammered copper: octagonal shaft and base made of fumed oak; bands and shade support of copper; height to burner, 16½ in.; base 10½ in. octagon; shade of Japanese brown wicker lined with red or green silk; supplied with plug, silk cord and sockets for three electric bulbs. Price of lamp complete, $20.00.

No. 377. Oil lamp with willow bowl and copper fount. Shade, No. 669, of Japanese wicker; height of lamp to top of shade, 19 in.; height of willow bowl, 8 in.; diameter of willow bowl, 11 in. Price of lamp with shade, complete, $12.00. Price of shade, $4.00.

No. 262

Electric Lamp in Copper with Shade of Opalescent Glass and Copper Bands
Lamp Complete with Shade - $32.00
Price of Shade - - - - 10.00

Height of Lamp over all 22 in.
Diameter of Base 7 in.
Diameter of Shade 16 in.
Fitted for Three Electric Bulbs

No. 262

No. 625

Electric Lamp of Fumed Oak and Hammered Copper, Complete with Shade of Hammered Copper Cut into Fretwork Panels and Lined with Opalescent Glass - - - - - - $40.00
Complete with Shade of Japanese Wicker - - - $20.00

Octagonal Shaft and Base Made of Fumed Oak, Bands and Shade Support of Copper
Height to Saucer 16½ in
Base 10½ in.
Diameter of Shade 18 in.
Fitted for Three Electric Bulbs

No. 625

SHADE B   56

No. 56

ONE-LIGHT ELECTRIC DESK LAMP, HAMMERED COPPER OR BRASS . . . $6.00 FURNISHED WITH SHADE A OR B. STANDARD 10 IN. HIGH. 15 IN. HIGH OVER ALL. BASE 6½ IN. IN DIAMETER, SHADE 10 IN. IN DIAMETER, 5 IN. HIGH.

755

No. 755

SIX-LIGHT ELECTRIC LAMP $115.00 HAMMERED IRON. SHADE OF AMBER TINTED HAMMERED GLASS BOUND WITH HAMMERED COPPER. STANDARD 23⅝ IN. HIGH. 35 IN. HIGH OVER ALL. BASE 13⅜ IN. SQUARE. SHADE 27 IN. IN DIAMETER, 8 IN. HIGH.

51

No. 51

THREE-LIGHT ELECTRIC LAMP . $16.50 POTTERY STANDARD IN BLENDING TONES OF BROWN AND GREEN. 21 IN. HIGH OVER ALL. JAPANESE WICKER SHADE 18 IN. IN DIAMETER, 7 IN. HIGH.

233

No. 233

ELECTRIC CANDLESTICK . . . . $8.00 HAMMERED COPPER OR BRASS. STANDARD 9 IN. HIGH. 16 IN. HIGH OVER ALL. BASE 5 IN. IN DIAMETER. SILK SHADE IN ANY DESIRED COLOR. CANDLESTICK WITHOUT SHADE $5.00

TRADE-MARK REG'D   IN U.S. PATENT OFFICE

611

No. 611. Electric lamp in fumed oak and hammered copper, with shade of woven sweet grass; height of lamp from base to shade holder, 15 in.; diameter of base, 10 in.; diameter of shade, 12 in.; supplied complete for use with plug, 8 ft. silk cord and 32-candle power electric bulb; price complete, $9.00.

609

610

No. 609. Electric lamp, base of fumed oak, 7 in. in diameter; copper standard, 18 in. high; sweet grass shade, 9 in. in diameter; supplied with plug, silk cord and socket for electric bulb; price complete for use, $7.00.

No. 610. Electric lamp in fumed oak and hammered copper; slender shape; suitable for desk light; globe of crystal, amber or straw-colored opalescent glass; supplied with plug, silk cord and 16 candle power bulb; height of lamp, 18 in.; diameter, 3 in.; diameter of base, 7 in. Price, complete for use, $6.50.

No. 608. Electric table lamp; standard and lantern frame of hammered copper or wrought iron, set upon a base of fumed oak; lantern of crystal, amber or straw-colored opalescent glass; length of base, 12 in.; width, 7 in.; thickness, 7/8 in.; height of standard, 18 in.; lantern, 5½ in. square at bottom; supplied with plug, silk cord and socket for electric bulb. Price complete, in copper, $15.00; in iron, $12.50.

77

No. 77. Small candlestick, made only in brass; height, 4 in.; diameter at base, 4 in. Price, $1.00.

TRADE MARK REG'D IN U.S. PATENT OFFICE

SHADE B   56

No. 506
ONE-LIGHT ELECTRIC ROOF
LAMP $12.00
AMBER GLASS SHADE LINED WITH
WHITE OPAQUE GLASS, SET IN AN
ADJUSTABLE HAMMERED COPPER
FRAME
BASE 10½ IN. LONG, 8 IN. WIDE
HEIGHT OVER ALL 19 IN.
THIS LAMP IS INTENDED FOR DESK
OR TABLE USE, AND MAKES AN
EXCELLENT READING LAMP, AS THE
SHADE CAN BE TILTED TO ANY
ANGLE SO AS TO THROW THE LIGHT
ON ONE'S BOOK OR WORK. AT THE
SAME TIME THE EYES ARE
PROTECTED FROM DIRECT LIGHT
BY THE MELLOW GLASS PANELS

506

No. 56
ONE-LIGHT ELECTRIC DESK LAMP
HAMMERED COPPER OR BRASS $6.00
FURNISHED WITH SHADE A OR B
15 IN. HIGH OVER ALL
BASE 6½ IN. IN DIAMETER
SHADE 10 IN. IN DIAMETER, 5 IN.
HIGH

No. 56½
TWO-LIGHT ELECTRIC DESK LAMP
(SAME DESIGN AS NO. 56)
HAMMERED COPPER OR BRASS $8.00
FURNISHED WITH SHADE A OR B
20 IN. HIGH OVER ALL
BASE 8 IN. IN DIAMETER
SHADE 14 IN. IN DIAMETER, 6½ IN.
HIGH

No. 503
ONE-LIGHT ELECTRIC LAMP $3.95
FURNISHED WITH SHADE A OR B
FUMED OAK STANDARD WITH BASE
5¼ IN. SQUARE
SHADE 10 IN. IN DIAMETER, 5 IN.
HIGH
HEIGHT OVER ALL 15 IN.

No. 500
ONE-LIGHT ELECTRIC LAMP $12.00
OAK STANDARD WITH HAMMERED
COPPER OR BRASS BANDS AND
FRAME SUPPORTING THE SHADE.
ADJUSTABLE SILK SHADE LINED
WITH WHITE LINEN.
SPREAD OF LAMP AT BASE 14 IN.
SHADE 10 IN. IN DIAMETER AND 5
IN. HIGH
THIS LAMP STANDS ON THE FLOOR
57 IN. HIGH OVER ALL.
IT IS ESPECIALLY SERVICEABLE AS A
READING LAMP, WHEN PLACED
BEHIND AN ARM CHAIR OR SETTLE
SO THAT THE LIGHT FALLS OVER
THE SHOULDER WITH A SOFT GLOW
THROUGH THE SILK SHADE

503

500

TRADE
MARK
REG'D
IN U.S.
PATENT
OFFICE

SHADE A

No. 500

PIANO LAMP
HAMMERED COPPER OR
BRASS $12.00
OAK STANDARD WITH
HAND-WROUGHT METAL
FRAME SUPPORTING THE
SHADE. ADJUSTABLE SILK
SHADE LINED WITH WHITE
LINEN. LAMP 5 FT. HIGH.
SHADE 9 IN. IN DIAMETER,
7 IN. HIGH.

58

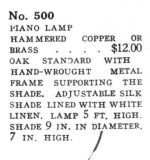

No. 58

ONE-LIGHT ELECTRIC
LAMP $5.75
FURNISHED WITH SHADE
A OR B. POTTERY STANDARD
9½ IN. HIGH. 14½ IN.
HIGH OVER ALL. BASE 5
IN. IN DIAMETER. SHADE
10 IN. IN DIAMETER, 5 IN.
HIGH.

506

No. 506

ONE-LIGHT ELECTRIC LAMP . . . $12.00
GREEN OR AMBER HAMMERED ANTIQUE
GLASS SHADE LINED WITH WHITE OPAQUE
GLASS, SET IN AN ADJUSTABLE HAMMERED
COPPER FRAME. 16½ IN. HIGH. 10½ IN.
LONG. BASE 9 IN. WIDE.

500

503
SHADE B

503
SHADE A

501

No. 503

ONE-LIGHT ELECTRIC
LAMP $3.95
FURNISHED WITH SHADE
A OR B. FUMED OAK
STANDARD 9 IN. HIGH. 14
IN. HIGH OVER ALL. BASE
5 IN. SQUARE. SHADE 10
IN. IN DIAMETER, 5 IN.
HIGH.

No. 501

ONE-LIGHT ELECTRIC DESK
LAMP $7.00
FUMED OAK STANDARD
UPON WHICH LAMP CAN
BE TILTED BACKWARD OR
FORWARD. SMALL SILK
SHADE OF GREEN OR ANY
OTHER PLAIN COLOR, LINED
WITH WHITE.

No. 57

ONE-LIGHT ELECTRIC LAMP . . . . . $5.75 FURNISHED WITH SHADE A OR B. POTTERY STANDARD 9½ IN. HIGH. 14½ IN. HIGH OVER ALL. BASE 5 IN. IN DIAMETER. SHADE 10 IN. IN DIAMETER, 5 IN. HIGH.

No. 505

TWO-LIGHT ELECTRIC LAMP . . . . . $7.80 FURNISHED WITH SHADE A OR B. FUMED OAK STANDARD 12 IN. HIGH, 1½ IN. SQUARE. 18½ IN. HIGH OVER ALL. BASE 6 IN. SQUARE. SHADE 14 IN. IN DIAMETER, 6½ IN. HIGH.

SHADE B

57

507

No. 294

OIL LAMP . . . $20.00 FURNISHED WITH JAPANESE SPLIT BAMBOO SHADE. HAMMERED COPPER OR BRASS, WROUGHT IRON HANDLES AND DECORATION. LAMP TO TOP OF BURNER 16 IN. HIGH.

294

SHADE B   505

No. 507

THREE-LIGHT ELECTRIC LAMP . . . . . $12.00 FURNISHED WITH SHADE A OR B. FUMED OAK STANDARD 14 IN. HIGH, 1¾ IN. SQUARE. 22 IN. HIGH OVER ALL. BASE 7½ IN. SQUARE. SHADE 18 IN. IN DIAMETER, 8 IN. HIGH.

No. 504

Electric Lamp with Shade of Japanese Wicker - - - - $12.00

Height 20 in.
Base 7½ in. x 7½ in.
Diameter of shade 17 in.
Fitted for Three Electric Bulbs

No. 504

TRADE-MARK REG'D IN U.S PATENT OFFICE

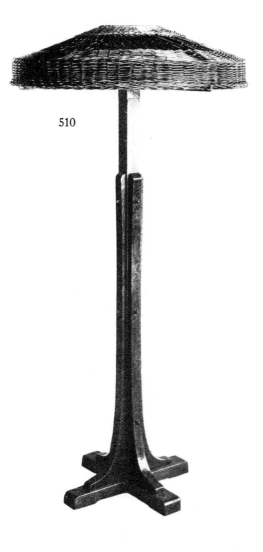

510

No. 510

HEIGHT OVER ALL 60 IN. (FROM FLOOR TO TOP OF SHADE). SIZE OF BASE 15½ IN. THE DIAMETER OF SHADE IS 31 IN. THE HEIGHT OF SHADE 8 IN. PRICE . . . . $26.00 WE CONSIDER THAT THIS LAMP IN BOTH STRUCTURE AND EFFECT IS ONE OF THE MOST SATISFACTORY THAT WE HAVE EVER BROUGHT OUT. THE STANDARD IS OF OAK, NATURAL TONE. THE SHADE IS OF WILLOW AND MAY BE LINED WITH ANY TONE OF SILK. IT MEASURES 32 IN. IN DIAMETER. IT IS AN EXCELLENT LAMP TO USE AT THE SIDE OF A PIANO OR AS A READING LAMP NEAR A COMFORTABLE ARM-CHAIR. IT IS FURNISHED WITH FOUR PULL-CHAIN BULBS WHICH THROW DOWN A POWERFUL, THOUGH BEAUTIFULLY DIFFUSED LIGHT.

541

No. 541

THREE-LIGHT ELECTRIC LAMP . . . . . . $15.00 FURNISHED WITH SHADE B. STANDARD 18 IN. HIGH, 27 IN. HIGH OVER ALL. SPREAD OF BASE 12 IN. SHADE 22 IN. IN DIAMETER, 9 IN. HIGH.

THESE Craftsman lamp shades are one of the most distinctive features of our lighting fixtures. They were originally intended for table lamps, either electric or oil, but we found them equally appropriate for ceiling lamps and for bracket fixtures on the side walls.

They are made for us in Japan from our own designs, of firmly woven willow lined with a heavy grade of Habutai silk in soft rich shades of red, green or dull gold, through which a mellow light is diffused.

The shades can be purchased separately as shown here, or with the lamps shown on other pages.

A-22

No. A-18
LAMP SHADE $2.50
JAPANESE WILLOW, LINED WITH SILK
18 IN. IN DIAMETER, 7½ IN. HIGH

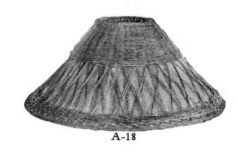

A-18

No. A-22
LAMP SHADE $3.25
JAPANESE WILLOW, LINED WITH SILK
22 IN. IN DIAMETFR, 9 IN. HIGH

No. A-10
LAMP SHADE $1.25
JAPANESE WILLOW, LINED WITH SILK
10 IN. IN DIAMETER, 4¾ IN. HIGH

A-14

No. A-14
LAMP SHADE $1.75
JAPANESE WILLOW, LINED WITH SILK
14 IN. IN DIAMETER 6½ IN. HIGH

A-10

TRADE- IN U.S.
MARK PATENT
REG'D OFFICE

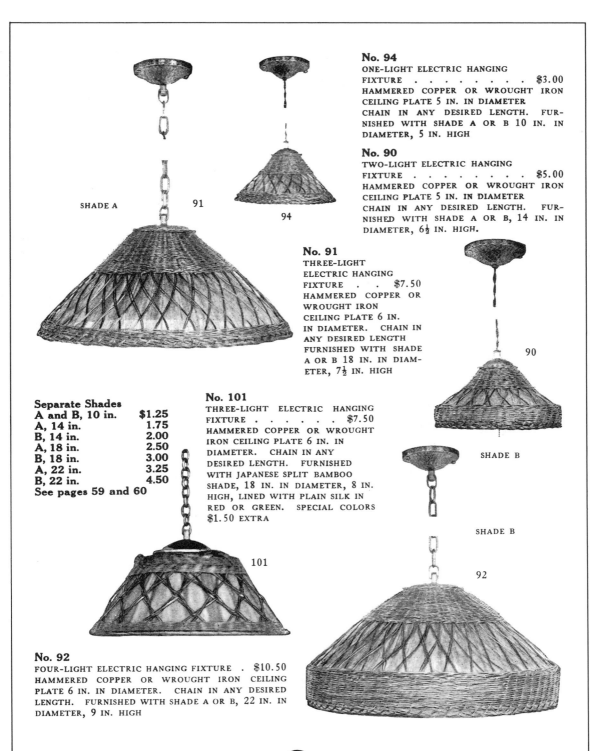

No. 94
ONE-LIGHT ELECTRIC HANGING
FIXTURE $3.00
HAMMERED COPPER OR WROUGHT IRON
CEILING PLATE 5 IN. IN DIAMETER
CHAIN IN ANY DESIRED LENGTH. FUR-
NISHED WITH SHADE A OR B 10 IN. IN
DIAMETER, 5 IN. HIGH

No. 90
TWO-LIGHT ELECTRIC HANGING
FIXTURE $5.00
HAMMERED COPPER OR WROUGHT IRON
CEILING PLATE 5 IN. IN DIAMETER
CHAIN IN ANY DESIRED LENGTH. FUR-
NISHED WITH SHADE A OR B, 14 IN. IN
DIAMETER, 6½ IN. HIGH.

No. 91
THREE-LIGHT
ELECTRIC HANGING
FIXTURE . . $7.50
HAMMERED COPPER OR
WROUGHT IRON
CEILING PLATE 6 IN.
IN DIAMETER. CHAIN IN
ANY DESIRED LENGTH
FURNISHED WITH SHADE
A OR B 18 IN. IN DIAM-
ETER, 7½ IN. HIGH

SHADE A   91

94

90

SHADE B

Separate Shades

Shade		
A and B, 10 in.	$1.25
A, 14 in.	1.75
B, 14 in.	2.00
A, 18 in.	2.50
B, 18 in.	3.00
A, 22 in.	3.25
B, 22 in.	4.50

See pages 59 and 60

No. 101
THREE-LIGHT ELECTRIC HANGING
FIXTURE $7.50
HAMMERED COPPER OR WROUGHT
IRON CEILING PLATE 6 IN. IN
DIAMETER. CHAIN IN ANY
DESIRED LENGTH. FURNISHED
WITH JAPANESE SPLIT BAMBOO
SHADE, 18 IN. IN DIAMETER, 8 IN.
HIGH, LINED WITH PLAIN SILK IN
RED OR GREEN. SPECIAL COLORS
$1.50 EXTRA

SHADE B

101

92

No. 92
FOUR-LIGHT ELECTRIC HANGING FIXTURE . $10.50
HAMMERED COPPER OR WROUGHT IRON CEILING
PLATE 6 IN. IN DIAMETER. CHAIN IN ANY DESIRED
LENGTH. FURNISHED WITH SHADE A OR B, 22 IN. IN
DIAMETER, 9 IN. HIGH

TRADE MARK REG'D   IN U.S PATENT OFFICE

No. 594. Three-light electrolier with chains of wrought iron and canopies of hammered copper, brass or wrought iron, on a fumed oak ceiling plate; lanterns are our regular No. 205, also made with bell-shaped globe, as shown in No. 592. Price, in copper or brass with lanterns, $18.50; in iron with lanterns, $16.00; in copper or brass with bells, $14.00; in iron with bells, $12.50.

No. 595. Nine-light electrolier, same design as No. 594. Price, in copper or brass with lanterns, $52.00; in iron with lanterns, $46.00; in copper or brass with bells, $34.00; in iron with bells, $31.00.

No. 598. Two-light electrolier; canopy and lanterns made in hammered copper, brass or wrought iron; bar and chains made always in wrought iron; oak ceiling plate 9 in. square, with metal canopy 6 in. square; bar, 14 in. long by 2 in. wide; lanterns, 7 in. high and 3½ in. square at the base, with globe of amber glass. Price, in copper or brass, $16.00; in iron, $14.00.

TRADE MARK REG'D IN U.S. PATENT OFFICE

No. 733

Five-Light Electrolier,
in Copper or Brass - $50.00
Iron and Copper - - 48.00
Iron - - - - - - 45.00

Diameter of Band 26 in.
Width of Band 4 in.
Height of Lanterns 10 in.
Diameter of Lanterns 4 in.
Lanterns furnished with Opalescent, Crystal or Amber Glass.
Supplied with Chain and Canopy

No. 599. Electrolier with five incandescent lights and four candles; made in hammered copper; band and supports of hammered copper; band, 5 in. wide and 24 in. square with candlesticks set at the corners; the lanterns used are our regular No. 671; chains of wrought iron; ceiling plate of oak 9 in. square, with copper canopy 6 in. square. Price, $58.00.

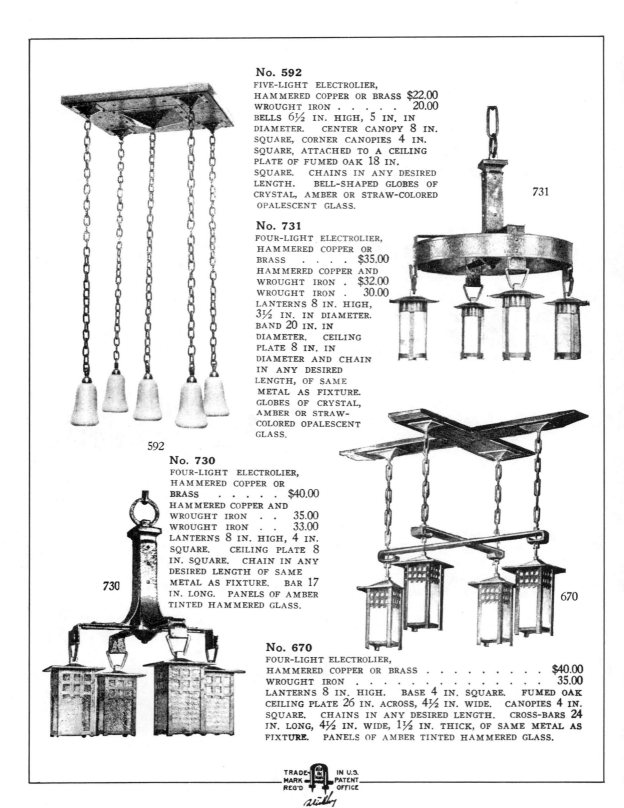

No. 592

FIVE-LIGHT ELECTROLIER, HAMMERED COPPER OR BRASS $22.00 WROUGHT IRON . . . . . 20.00 BELLS 6½ IN. HIGH, 5 IN. IN DIAMETER. CENTER CANOPY 8 IN. SQUARE, CORNER CANOPIES 4 IN. SQUARE, ATTACHED TO A CEILING PLATE OF FUMED OAK 18 IN. SQUARE. CHAINS IN ANY DESIRED LENGTH. BELL-SHAPED GLOBES OF CRYSTAL, AMBER OR STRAW-COLORED OPALESCENT GLASS.

731

No. 731

FOUR-LIGHT ELECTROLIER, HAMMERED COPPER OR BRASS . . . $35.00 HAMMERED COPPER AND WROUGHT IRON . $32.00 WROUGHT IRON . 30.00 LANTERNS 8 IN. HIGH, 3½ IN. IN DIAMETER. BAND 20 IN. IN DIAMETER. CEILING PLATE 8 IN. IN DIAMETER AND CHAIN IN ANY DESIRED LENGTH, OF SAME METAL AS FIXTURE. GLOBES OF CRYSTAL, AMBER OR STRAW-COLORED OPALESCENT GLASS.

592

No. 730

FOUR-LIGHT ELECTROLIER, HAMMERED COPPER OR BRASS . . . . $40.00 HAMMERED COPPER AND WROUGHT IRON . . 35.00 WROUGHT IRON . . 33.00 LANTERNS 8 IN. HIGH, 4 IN. SQUARE. CEILING PLATE 8 IN. SQUARE. CHAIN IN ANY DESIRED LENGTH OF SAME METAL AS FIXTURE. BAR 17 IN. LONG. PANELS OF AMBER TINTED HAMMERED GLASS.

730

670

No. 670

FOUR-LIGHT ELECTROLIER, HAMMERED COPPER OR BRASS . . . . $40.00 WROUGHT IRON . . . . 35.00 LANTERNS 8 IN. HIGH. BASE 4 IN. SQUARE. FUMED OAK CEILING PLATE 26 IN. ACROSS, 4½ IN. WIDE. CANOPIES 4 IN. SQUARE. CHAINS IN ANY DESIRED LENGTH. CROSS-BARS 24 IN. LONG, 4½ IN. WIDE, 1½ IN. THICK, OF SAME METAL AS FIXTURE. PANELS OF AMBER TINTED HAMMERED GLASS.

TRADE-MARK REG'D IN U.S. PATENT OFFICE

590

Nos. 590 and 592

Five-Light Electroliers, made with wrought iron chains, and canopies of hammered copper, brass, or iron attached to a ceiling plate of fumed oak. Bell-shaped globes in crystal, amber or straw-colored opalescent glass. Also made with lanterns

Nos. 591 and 593

Nine-Light Electrolier (Same Design as No. 590)

In Copper or Brass, with Bells - - - - - - - -	$38.00
In Iron, with Bells - - -	35.00
In Copper or Brass, with Lanterns - - - - - -	56.00
In Iron, with Lanterns - -	52.00

No. 764

Dome, in Copper or Brass - - - - - -	$90.00
In Iron - - - - - -	87.00

Six amber tinted hammered bent glass panels in dome, with 18 small glass panels, 5 in. square, bound in metal, swinging loose from the metal rim of the dome
Diameter of Dome 26 in.
Fitted for four electric lights
Three candle brackets for use in emergency
Supplied with Chain and Canopy

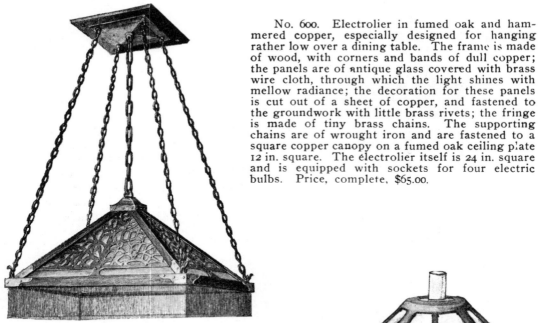

No. 600. Electrolier in fumed oak and hammered copper, especially designed for hanging rather low over a dining table. The frame is made of wood, with corners and bands of dull copper; the panels are of antique glass covered with brass wire cloth, through which the light shines with mellow radiance; the decoration for these panels is cut out of a sheet of copper, and fastened to the groundwork with little brass rivets; the fringe is made of tiny brass chains. The supporting chains are of wrought iron and are fastened to a square copper canopy on a fumed oak ceiling plate 12 in. square. The electrolier itself is 24 in. square and is equipped with sockets for four electric bulbs. Price, complete, $65.00.

No. 600.

No. 290. Oil lamp with fount of brass or hammered copper in frame of wrought iron; shade of brass or copper with panels of mica and fringe of tiny brass chains; height of lamp to top of shade, 24 in.; shade, 16 in. in diameter, 8 in. deep; fount, 5 in. in diameter; standards, 1 in. wide and ⅛ in. thick. Price, $18.00.

No. 291. Hanging oil lamp; made in hammered copper or brass, with chains of wrought iron; round ceiling plate of oak with canopy of copper or brass; shade of copper or brass with mica panels, 20 in. in diameter, 8 in deep, with fringe of tiny brass chains; fount, 5 in. in diameter. Price, in copper or brass, $20.00.

No. 777

Electric Lantern, complete with canopy and chain of same metal as lantern, in Copper or Brass - - - - - - - - $25.00

Height of Lantern 14 in.
Base 7 in. square
Mosaic Favrile Glass Panels

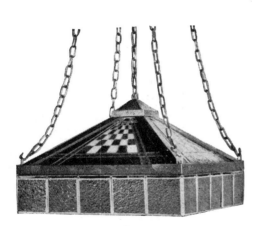

No. 760

Dome, Copper or Brass
Trim - - - - - $78.00
Iron Trim - - - 75.00

Dome 8 in. deep, 24 in. square, fumed oak frame with mosaic favrile glass. Swinging panels of amber tinted hammered glass, 4¾ in. square, bound in metal. Fitted for four electric lights. Supplied complete with chain and canopy

No. 750

Dome, Panels of Amber Tinted Hammered Glass, framed in Copper - $40.00
Iron and Copper - 38.00
Iron - - - - - 35.00

Dome 6 in. deep, 20 in. square, panels of amber tinted hammered glass, 5 in. square, bound in metal, swinging loose from rim. Fitted for four electric lights. Supplied complete with chain and canopy

TRADE-MARK REG'D — IN U.S. PATENT OFFICE

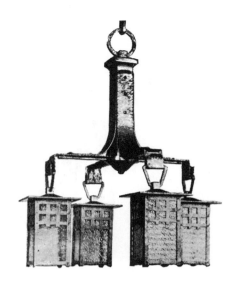

No. 730

Electrolier in Copper or
Brass - - - - - - $40.00
In Iron and Copper - - 35.00
In Iron - - - - - 33.00

Height of Lanterns 8 in.
Width of Lanterns 4 in.
Globe of Amber Tinted Hammered Glass
Width of Crossbars, 17 in.
Supplied with Chain and Canopy

540

No. 540
ELECTRIC HANGING
WILLOW FIXTURE . . $28.00
THIS FIXTURE HAS FIVE BULBS,
FOUR DIFFUSING LIGHT THROUGH
THE SILK-LINED SHADE AND THE
WILLOW WORK. ONE SENDS
DOWN THE LIGHT DIRECTLY
THROUGH A BOWL OF YELLOW
LEADED GLASS, INTENSIFYING
THE GLOW AT THIS POINT.
THE CHAINS FOR THIS FIXTURE
MAY BE LONG OR SHORT
ACCORDING TO ITS USE.
PLACED OVER A DINING TABLE
IT SHOULD BE FAIRLY LOW,
IN THE HALL CONSIDERABLY
HIGHER. IT IS AN EXCEPTIONAL
LIGHT FOR ANY SORT
OF TABLE, AS AT NO
ANGLE ARE THE BULBS
REVEALED.
SHADE 8 IN. HIGH,
31 IN. IN DIAMETER,
STAINED IN EITHER
BROWN OR GREEN AND
LINED WITH A HEAVY
HABUTAI SILK IN ANY
SHADE

TRADE MARK REG'D — IN U.S. PATENT OFFICE

202

No. 202

ELECTRIC PIANO DROP LIGHT, HAMMERED COPPER OR BRASS . . . . . $12.00 LANTERN 7 IN. HIGH, 6 IN. IN DIAMETER. BASE 7 IN. IN DIAMETER. PROJECTION 16½ IN.

No. 226

ONE-LIGHT ELECTRIC LANTERN HAMMERED COPPER OR BRASS $7.50 WROUGHT IRON . . . 6.75 LANTERN 7 IN. HIGH. BASE 3½ IN. IN DIAMETER. BRACKET 10¾ IN. HIGH, PROJECTION 9 IN. GLOBE OF CRYSTAL, AMBER OR STRAW-COLORED OPALESCENT GLASS.

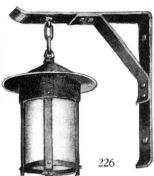

226

No. 515

ONE-LIGHT ELECTRIC LANTERN HAMMERED COPPER OR BRASS . $11.00 WROUGHT IRON . . $9.00 LANTERN 9½ IN. HIGH. TOP 6½ IN. SQUARE. BASE 5 IN. SQUARE. CEILING PLATE 6 IN. IN DIAMETER AND CHAIN ANY DESIRED LENGTH, BOTH SAME METAL AS LANTERN. PANELS OF AMBER TINTED HAMMERED GLASS. FITTED WITH GLASS DOOR AT BOTTOM.

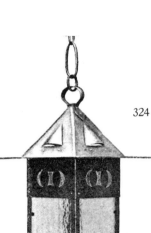

324

No. 304

ONE-LIGHT ELECTRIC LANTERN AND BRACKET, HAMMERED COPPER OR BRASS . . $10.00 WROUGHT IRON . . 8.00 LANTERN 10 IN. HIGH. BASE 4 IN. IN DIAMETER. CANOPY 5 IN. IN DIAMETER. PROJECTION OF BRACKET 6 IN. GLOBE OF CRYSTAL, AMBER OR STRAW-COLORED OPALESCENT GLASS.

No. 225

ONE-LIGHT ELECTRIC LANTERN AND BRACKET. SAME DESIGN AS NO. 304. HAMMERED COPPER OR BRASS $8.00 WROUGHT IRON . . . 7.00 LANTERN 8 IN. HIGH. BASE 3 IN. IN DIAMETER. CANOPY 5 IN. IN DIAMETER. PROJECTION OF BRACKET 6 IN.

No. 324

ONE-LIGHT ELECTRIC LANTERN HAMMERED COPPER OR BRASS $12.00 WROUGHT IRON . . . . . 9.50 LANTERN 15 IN. HIGH. TOP 9 IN. SQUARE. BASE 5½ IN. SQUARE. CEILING PLATE 6 IN. SQUARE AND CHAIN IN ANY DESIRED LENGTH OF SAME METAL AS LANTERN. PANELS OF AMBER TINTED HAMMERED GLASS.

304

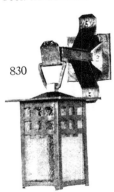

830

No. 830

ONE-LIGHT ELECTRIC LANTERN AND BRACKET, HAMMERED COPPER OR BRASS . . . . $11.50 HAMMERED COPPER AND WROUGHT IRON . . . 11.00 WROUGHT IRON . . . . 10.00 LANTERN 8 IN. HIGH. BASE 4 IN. SQUARE. WALL PLATE 8 IN. HIGH AND 2 IN. WIDE. PROJECTION OF BRACKET 7 IN. PANELS OF AMBER TINTED HAMMERED GLASS.

TRADE MARK REG'D — IN U.S. PATENT OFFICE

673

No. 671. Electric lantern of hammered copper, brass or wrought iron, complete with canopy of same metal as lantern and chain of wrought iron; height of lantern, 7 in.; base, 3½ in. square; canopy, 6 in. square; globe of amber glass. Price, with lantern of copper or brass, $7.50; of iron, $6.50.

No. 673. Electric lantern of hammered copper or wrought iron, with chain and canopy of wrought iron; globe of moulded edge glass; height of lantern, 7 in.; base, 5 in. square; canopy, 6 in. square. Complete with canopy of same metal as lantern and chain of wrought iron. Price, with lantern of copper, $10.00; of iron, $8.50.

671

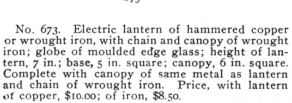

228

No. 513
ELECTRIC SCONCE
COMPLETE WITH MICA SHADE.
COPPER OR BRASS . $8 00
IRON $7 50
SCONCE 12 IN. HIGH, 6 IN. WIDE

PROJECTION OF BRACKET 6 IN.
BASE OF SHADE 4 IN.

513

No. 228. Side light with two lanterns; made in hammered copper, brass or wrought iron. The 6 in. square wall plate is of oak with a canopy of metal to which the scroll band is fastened. This band is 1¾ in. wide, 12 in. across and with a 5 in. projection. The lanterns are our regular No. 205. Price, in copper or brass, $14.00; in iron, $11.50.

No. 512
ELECTRIC SCONCE
(SAME DESIGN AND SIZE AS 513, BUT FITTED WITH TWO LIGHTS)
COPPER OR BRASS $12.00
IRON $11.00

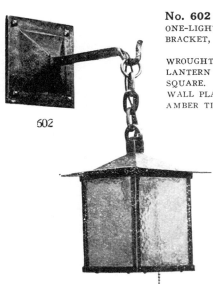

602

No. 602

ONE-LIGHT ELECTRIC LANTERN AND BRACKET, HAMMERED COPPER OR BRASS $10.00
WROUGHT IRON 7.50
LANTERN 6½ IN. HIGH. BASE 5 IN. SQUARE. PROJECTION OF BRACKET 8 IN. WALL PLATE 8 IN. SQUARE. PANELS OF AMBER TINTED HAMMERED GLASS.

400

No. 400

ELECTRIC BELL LIGHT WITH BRACKET, HAMMERED COPPER OR BRASS $4.50
WROUGHT IRON 3.75
GLOBE 6½ IN. HIGH. BASE 4¾ IN. IN DIAMETER. BRACKET 10 IN. HIGH, PROJECTION 8 IN. BELL-SHAPED GLOBE OF CRYSTAL, AMBER OR STRAW COLORED OPALESCENT GLASS.

No. 672

ONE-LIGHT ELECTRIC LANTERN, HAMMERED COPPER OR BRASS $9.00
WROUGHT IRON 7.50
LANTERN 7 IN. HIGH. BASE 4½ IN. SQUARE. CEILING PLATE 6 IN. SQUARE AND CHAIN OF ANY DESIRED LENGTH IN SAME METAL AS LANTERN. PANELS OF AMBER TINTED HAMMERED GLASS.

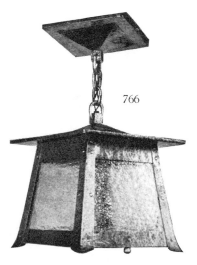

766

No. 766

ONE-LIGHT ELECTRIC LANTERN HAMMERED COPPER OR BRASS $18.00
WROUGHT IRON . . 16.00
LANTERN 16 IN. HIGH. BASE 12 IN. SQUARE. CEILING PLATE AND CHAIN IN ANY DESIRED LENGTH OF SAME METAL AS LANTERN. PANELS OF AMBER TINTED HAMMERED GLASS. FITTED WITH GLASS DOOR AT BOTTOM.

672

No. 509

ONE-LIGHT ELECTRIC LANTERN AND BRACKET, HAMMERED COPPER OR BRASS $8.00
WROUGHT IRON 7.00
LANTERN 7 IN. HIGH. BASE 4½ IN. SQUARE, BRACKET 10½ IN. HIGH, PROJECTION 7 IN. PANELS OF AMBER TINTED HAMMERED GLASS, 4½ IN. SQUARE, BOUND IN METAL SWINGING LOOSE FROM RIM.

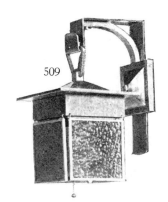

509

TRADE MARK REG'D   IN U.S. PATENT OFFICE

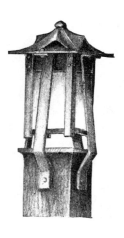

No. 70. Candlestick made in hammered copper or brass; height, 12 in.; base, 5 in. square; top, 2 in. square. Price, $4.00.

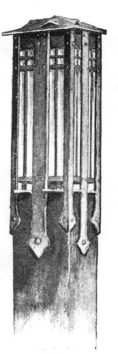

No. 701

ONE-LIGHT ELECTRIC NEWEL POST LAMP, HAMMERED COPPER OR BRASS $15.00
WROUGHT IRON . . . 13.00
LANTERN 9 IN. HIGH. BASE 4 IN. SQUARE. PANELS OF AMBER TINTED HAMMERED GLASS.

No. 703

ONE-LIGHT ELECTRIC NEWEL POST LAMP
HAMMERED COPPER OR BRASS . . . $20.00
WROUGHT IRON 17.50
LANTERN 14 IN. HIGH, BASE 6 IN. SQUARE.
PANELS OF AMBER OR CRYSTAL LEADED GLASS.

703

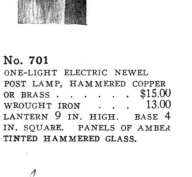

70

No. 297

CANDLE SCONCE, SCROLL DESIGN, HAMMERED COPPER OR BRASS $3.00
WROUGHT IRON 2.25
13 IN. HIGH. 3 IN. WIDE.

No. 76

CANDLE BRACKET, HAMMERED COPPER OR BRASS $2.00
WROUGHT IRON . 1.50
11 IN. HIGH.

No. 75

SAME DESIGN AS NO. 76. HAMMERED COPPER OR BRASS $1.50
WROUGHT IRON . 1.25
9 IN. HIGH.

No. 74

CANDLESTICK, HAMMERED COPPER OR BRASS . . $2.50
WROUGHT IRON 2.25
9 IN. HIGH. SAUCER 7½ IN. IN DIAMETER. SHAFT 1½ IN. IN DIAMETER.

74

76

297

83

702

No. 83

SCREEN, PANELED IN JAPANESE
GRASS CLOTH . . . $18.00
PANELED IN CRAFTSMAN
CANVAS $22.00
66 IN. HIGH
THREE PANELS EACH 22 IN. WIDE

No. 702

NEWEL POST LAMP IN COPPER
OR BRASS $12.00
IRON $10.50
LANTERN 8 IN. HIGH
BASE 4 IN. SQUARE
AMBER TINTED HAMMERED
GLASS

No. 84

SCREEN $24.00
WOOD PANELS. 66 IN. HIGH
THREE PANELS EACH 22 IN. WIDE

No. 91

SCREEN, SHEEPSKIN PANELS $26.00
68 IN. HIGH. THREE PANELS EACH 22 IN. WIDE

91

84

Inlaid Oak Music Cabinet, designed by Harvey Ellis and executed by Gustav Stickley

Als
ik
kan